M000015134

The Dilemma Of Love

Healing Co-dependent Relationships At Different Stages Of Life

Susan Cooley Ricketson, Ph.D.

Health Communications, Inc.
Deerfield Beach, Florida

Library of Congress Cataloging-in-Publication Data

Ricketson, Susan Cooley.
  The dilemma of love : healing co-dependent relationships
at different stages of life / Susan Cooley Ricketson.
      p.   cm.
  Includes bibliographical references.
  ISBN 1-55874-051-1
  1. Co-dependence (Psychology)   I. Title.
  RC569.5.C63R53   1989   89-39155
  616.86—dc20   CIP

©1989 Susan Cooley Ricketson

ISBN 1-55874-051-1

All rights reserved. Printed in the United States of America. No
part of this publication may be reproduced, stored in a retrieval
system or transmitted in any form or by any means, electronic,
mechanical, photocopying, recording or otherwise without the
written permission of the publisher.

Publisher: Health Communications, Inc.
          3201 S.W. 15th Street
          Deerfield Beach, Florida 33442

Cover designer: Reta Thomas

ACKNOWLEDGMENTS

I would like to acknowledge my editors, Jerry Ackerman and David Thurston.

In recognition of Christine Pieper for her support throughout this project.

Wayne Kritsberg and Dr. Joan Kenley for their encouragement, guidance and generosity from the onset of this project.

Pinny Bugaeff for reading the first full manuscript and giving feedback and loving support.

Kathy Peterson and Donna Robuck for reading portions of my manuscript and offering feedback and encouragement.

To Evelyn Andrews and Lynn Collins for their close personal sharing through my process of writing the book.

To all my beautiful friends who have been so patient with me through this process.

My dear friends in A.W.I. who are a special family to me.

My extended family in Ohio, each of whom I love in a very special way.

My mother, Pauline Hines Schmitkons, who has been with me in spirit since her transition in 1966.

My father, George Edwin Schmitkons and my step-mother Rose Spindler Schmitkons. They have each given me inspiration in their own unique way.

My brother, Stephen, and my sister, Virginia, who were taken from us in childhood because of a tragedy but whose spirits I remain in touch with.

Special regard to Elizabeth Cooley Earling who has been a mother to me for nearly three decades.

My husband, Brad, who has been a real friend.

My children Rex, Caroline and Katherine Cooley.

My stepsons Peter, Stephen, Paul and David Ricketson.

And to all my clients, past and present. They are all precious to me.

The personal stories in this book are based on real people. The stories have been altered when necessary and the names changed to protect privacy.

"Trager" and "Mentastics" are registered service marks of the Trager Institute, and are used with permission of the Trager Institute.

The case material on chronic shock appeared in an article by the author in the Trager® Newsletter, February, 1989, Vol VIII, No. 1.

(Kurn Robins)

CONTENTS

(Kumiko Amino)

PREFACE

This book is about reclaiming your birthright to love and be loved. It is about waking up. You have a right to be a fully present human being. You have a right to look to each day as a challenge and an adventure. You have a right to share in this adventure with other healthy supportive people. This can be your life, and this book can guide you as you start, and continue, on the road to more consciousness and more awareness of who you really are.

I believe that the key to your freedom in the present is learning about, and healing from, your past. As you do this, you will become more aware of what you do and why you do it, and you will be able to make healthy choices for yourself.

You are not a robot who must do things because they have been done a certain way for generations. You may say, "Well, this is just the way I am" or "That is just the way he or she is." But it doesn't have to be that way forever.

You can change. You can begin to understand yourself and your motives. You can learn to handle situations differently if you are not pleased with the way things are now. You are a unique human being who can live with dignity, integrity and respect for the rights of others. You can follow your spirit and fill your world with love, and support those around you to do the same.

I have always been interested in families. I see families as fascinating connections between people. I say this not as a person living on Cloud Nine of the American Dream, but as someone who knows only too well — from personal experience and from years working as a therapist — how traumatic life in a family can be when touched deeply by death, divorce, mental problems, alcoholism and unresolved conflicts between spouses, children, parents and grandparents.

You may think of your family in many ways. When I think of mine, I think mostly of all the ways in which we cared and were cared for. I am struck by how difficult, if not impossible, this caring often was. I have since learned that, through the generations, families pass along patterns of loving — as well as patterns of abusing and neglecting — in the same way they pass along their values, rules and culture. These patterns of loving often become distorted and harmful to the members of the family.

Look around and you will see, perhaps in your own life and the lives of others, incident after incident of parents who neglect and emotionally and physically abuse their children. You will see alcoholism, drug problems and other kinds of dysfunction running through the generations. At the other end of life, you will see many elderly parents feeling abandoned, depending more upon the care of strangers than their own children.

Marge, a mother in her late 30s, once told me, "I dread the thought of my parents getting sick or disabled. I can barely deal with them now for longer than five minutes at a time. They try to run my life. They criticize everything I do. How could I cope with taking care of them? Then I think about myself and when I get older. The last thing in the world I want is for my kids to feel that way about *me*."

In this book we will look at how, as in Marge's experience, things get turned upside down in many families. If parents are alcoholic or dysfunctional, they are unable to care for themselves and their children in healthy ways. Children learn self-destructive methods to cope with such situations, and they learn to take care of their parents on an emotional level. This is how children become co-dependent.

Essentially, co-dependents look to other people and external things to fill the emptiness they feel inside, to give them a feeling of self-worth. By focusing outside of themselves they deny their needs and their own problems.

You may have taken care of your parents emotionally when you were an infant and young child. Today you may still be taking care of your parents in inappropriate ways. We will see how these patterns of attachment and caring for your parents affect you at different stages of your life: growing up, finding a path in life, getting married, having children of your own then coping with your parents' old age and deaths. You can begin to disentangle the threads of love, guilt and fear that bind you to your parents, and you can learn the difference between co-dependency and true caring.

It is my hope that you can build what Sharon Wegscheider-Cruse calls a *Family of Choice* to support you as you learn how to understand and make the most of your *Family of Chance*. Your Family of Chance is the one into which you were born. Your Family of Choice is made up of friends who develop into a support network to help you become a full person. With support from your new family, the one you choose in recovery, you can regain the love that you were born with and possibly bring this love back to your original family — to the people who brought you into the world.

In the first days of my own recovery, I found this quote on a bookmark:

> I shall pass through this world but once. If, therefore, there be any kindness I can show, or any good I can do let me do it now. Let me not defer or neglect it for I shall not pass this way again.

> Etienne de Grellet

When my co-dependency conned me into believing that I did not matter, this quote helped me see that I *did* count

and my sharing was worthwhile. I had not lost my desire
to connect with the spirit of others. I believe that opening
up to the love within me was essential to bringing me to
where I am today. From the beginning I have sensed that
it is love, connectedness and caring that make life worthwhile, and that the key to recovery from co-dependency is
learning to live from your true self so that this love can be
shared freely with others.

I hope this book touches you as this quote touched me.
When you read the book, take from it what resonates
within you and let the rest go. If you can, try to suspend
judgment and take in those parts with which you can
identify. A year from now you may want to read the book
again. You may find that different issues resonate within
you in the future.

As you take steps to understand your disease and share
your recovery with others, you may find that your love
for yourself and for the people in your life will grow. So
much of what is meant by recovery is the opening of your
once closed and hurt heart, not only to the little child ·
within yourself, but to that child within all of us.

PART
I

The Dilemma
Of Love

1

The Dilemma Of Love

I have a simple question for you: *What is love?*

How do you love someone, anyone — a friend, a spouse, a child, your parents? What do you do? How do you show your love? How much of yourself do you give to another person? How does it feel to care for someone? Is love a relaxing, liberating feeling, a warm urge to share yourself with another? Or is love a confusing struggle that always leaves someone hurt?

People have asked these questions for thousands of years. Although we may never know all the answers, I hope that this book can help you begin to understand the vital, joyful sense of love that is every person's birthright. I hope that you can begin to see that healthy love is quite different from what I believe is the skewed sense of love that is prevalent in our society.

For the past 15 years I have been exploring how to free my inner spirit to live to my fullest and feel true empathy for myself and for others. Before I started my recovery, I was aware that something did not feel right inside me.

In the past few years there has finally emerged a name for what had interfered with so much of my life: co-dependency.

What Is Co-dependency?

Co-dependency is a disease brought on by growing up in a dysfunctional family. When your parents are unable to be fully present to you because they are unable to be fully present to themselves and each other, you can be deeply affected. You grow up without being shown how to love with openness and spontaneity. You gradually turn off your ability to be fully alive.

This process can take place subtly, much like water eroding a rock little by little. Eventually you adapt by burying your heart and denying that you need your parents' love. You learn to physically and emotionally take care of your parents. As you grow up, your true self becomes buried deeper, and you become further removed from your loving spirit. When you are an adult you may face life wondering what love is, whether it is possible to love anyone and whether love even exists.

The doubts and concerns of the following clients reflect the harm that co-dependency can cause in people's lives:

- "Did my parents really love me? Really care for me? If they really loved me, why didn't they treat me with more dignity and caring? Why were they so distant, so self-absorbed and sometimes even abusive and violent?"
- "I got burned growing up. My family hurt me so much, why should I give anyone else a chance to hurt me again?"
- "Nobody really knows or cares about me. Why should I care about anyone else?"
- "What's the point of trying to help anyone? I feel drained and my help is never enough. I can't fix the problem and people just get mad at me for interfering."
- "How can I believe I'm a loving person when I know I've hurt people and have selfish desires?"

- "Is there any place in this world for a loving, caring heart? Isn't empathy a sign of weakness, and don't the weak always get hurt and used?"
- "Is being intimate something I can learn or am I doomed to be alone for the rest of my life?"
- "It's impossible to have a good relationship. I give them my heart, but they want my soul."

These statements may sound familiar to you. You may have heard them said, or said them yourself. They reflect what I call the *Dilemma of Love:*

> Co-dependents learn that feeling love for others often leads to disease and self-destructiveness, yet no recovery can be full or meaningful without reawakening your loving nature.

All of us who have suffered from co-dependency and addictions need to rediscover what it means to love. *Empathy* is defined as *identification with and understanding of another's situation, feelings and motives.* It means being fully present with someone while he or she is feeling, and being able to stay with that person's feelings. When you are empathetic you do not try to "fix" someone, make the person's emotions go away or interfere with the healing process. You support another's healing process by simply *being present.* It is important that you are able to do this for yourself also.

Matt was skeptical about empathy because he felt he already revolved too much around his mother's needs. He did whatever his mother wanted and always tried to guess at what she was feeling. He was so busy paying attention to what his mother might need that he never learned to be aware of his own needs. In fact, he did not even know he had needs.

In therapy Matt had to learn to feel his own feelings and identify his own needs. He discovered that his efforts to try to please his mother were rooted in his unconscious fear of abandonment and, therefore, were not an expression of healthy empathy. Because Matt's mother had not shared her feelings with him, he had not been taught to have a true sensitivity to people's feelings. Matt had never been given the opportunity to truly listen when someone was sharing and to try to understand how it felt to be in another's shoes.

If you are co-dependent, you may wish for love with all your heart or feel threatened by love and run away from it. You may think of love as painful, as suffocating, as an unreachable dream. If you were raised in a dysfunctional home, it is only natural that you would doubt that true love for yourself and others is possible.

Healthy love *is* possible for you and for anyone who chooses to recover from co-dependency. Recovery takes time and a commitment to look honestly at your past and at yourself. It is a difficult process at times. If you can be gentle with yourself and let others support you along your journey, you can become free.

To find your way out of co-dependency, it helps to know how you got into it in the first place — it helps to understand the roots of your co-dependency.

How Children Take Care Of Their Parents

Many times parents are emotionally unavailable to themselves and their families because they have not resolved the issues from their own troubled childhoods. As a result of their upbringings, parents can suffer from the disease of co-dependency from which spring addictions, such as alcoholism, drug addiction, workaholism, sexual addiction, love addiction or eating disorders and compulsive caretaking to name a few. Without treatment, these problems live on and carry over into the lives of the children. This is called *multigenerational transmission of disease.*

Parents do not usually pass their diseases on to children on purpose. Many parents, in fact, strive to raise their children differently from the way they were raised — vowing to give their children a life better than they had.

Unfortunately, parents are often not conscious of their negative patterns of behaving and thinking. This is the tragic nature of these diseases. The person suffers without being aware that he or she has a disease and, therefore, does not take steps to heal from it.

When parents fail to get the appropriate help they need, they often act out the basic dynamics of an unhealthy family.

Parents unconsciously expect their children to help them cope with the unresolved issues of their own childhoods.

When parents suffer from alcoholism or any of the other "isms," their marriage is usually rocky and unfulfilling. If a parent is not on good terms with his or her spouse, often the next closest person to turn to is a child.

Hugh described to me a typical weekend at home as a child. "On Friday night, my dad would come home drunk and start yelling as soon as he came in the door. My mother would try to calm him down, but he would only get more abusive. They would fight and finally he would storm out of the house. He would stay away all weekend without telling my mother where he was. My mother would be miserable and come into my room to tell me that she couldn't stand it anymore. I was just 10 years old, but I figured I was the only one she had to talk to. I would listen and try to cheer her up, staying in the whole weekend to be sure she was all right. I figured that's what you do when you really love someone."

When you learn to take care of your parents you gradually repress your feelings. You see the stress your parents are under, so you do what you can to keep them from becoming nervous and upset. Some feelings may be allowed in your family. For instance, you may get attention if you act sad and helpless. Usually, though, feelings of anger or frustration are unacceptable. When you know these feelings are unacceptable to your family, you gradually convince yourself that you never get angry or upset.

As a child your efforts to take care of your parents take on a particular urgency. You fear that if your parents get sick, they may die then you will die also. Your fear of loss drives you to try to help your parents at great cost to your own personal growth.

Family Systems And Caring

As a child when you struggle to rescue a parent, you are involved with more than just the parent's disease. You operate within the context of a whole family.

Families are complex entities. In her book *Another Chance*, Sharon Wegscheider-Cruse compares a family to a mobile: The members of a family affect each other in everything they do. The mobile stays in balance when each member contributes his or her part to the whole. In this sense, a family operates as a system.

In a healthy family system you are taught skills as a child to cope in all areas of life. Some of these areas are:

- **Relationship with self:** learning to love and respect yourself, learning to be responsible for your life without excessive control or compulsion.
- **Interpersonal life:** learning to relate to other people in healthy ways in which the spiritual integrity of each person is maintained.
- **Spiritual life:** gaining a trust in a Spiritual Force in the universe that is beyond the power of you and your parents.
- **Emotional life:** learning to honor your feelings and share them appropriately with others.
- **Mental life:** learning to use your mental capacities in a balanced way to solve problems.
- **Physical challenges:** learning to ride a bicycle, build a treehouse, etc.

When you are supported to grow in these areas, you can become your own person and contribute your unique qualities to the family system.

In a healthy family system, each member is honored as an individual within the system. There is room for each person to express feelings and to be fully alive. As Bob Earll says,

"A functional family is one built on a foundation of love and mutual trust. The parents have a good sense of self. They are in touch with feelings. They are able to express their feelings openly. They are able to let their children express their feelings openly. They are emotionally available for their children. There is an abundance of physical contact, holding, hugging. Rigidity and conformity are discouraged. The uniqueness of each child is encouraged. The parents have clearly defined limits and boundaries. Limits: how far they will go. Boundaries: how far they will let you go."

I Got Tired of Pretending

When a family is healthy, the roles members play and the family rules and expectations do not confine the parents or the children. They only serve as useful guidelines.

For instance, a healthy family may enjoy certain rituals every Christmas. It may make a point of having all its members together on Christmas Eve to decorate the house and trim the Christmas tree. If you are a son in this family and you receive an invitation to a special Christmas Eve ball, the family adjusts to this change. Your parents may ask you to be with the family for a short time before you leave for the ball, but they accept that you are growing older, and that you will have more interests outside of the family.

This flexibility is not possible in a dysfunctional home. When a family lives with a disease such as co-dependency or alcoholism, the family adjusts and focuses its concern on the sick member. When the stress on the family becomes too great, the balance in the family system is thrown off. All of the family's energy is directed towards the sick member. There is no room left within the system for others in the family to have needs and to explore their individuality. In time the family becomes a dysfunctional system: Its rules and customs become rigid and damaging to the individuals, especially to the children.

In a dysfunctional family system if you want to go out on Christmas Eve instead of staying home the entire evening to participate in the family tradition, the family feels threatened and abandoned. You are needed to help carry the burden of the troubled family. There is no room for flexibility and negotiation.

In response to the problems in your family, you learn to bury your feelings and your needs. Often without being asked, you will do what the family demands of you. You play your role flawlessly, obey the rules, stay loyal to the family and anticipate what the family expects of you.

In this way you take care of more than your parents. You try to take care of a whole family system. The same fear which leads you to rescue a sick parent drives you to take care of the whole family. The thought of losing a parent to sickness is frightening to a child, but the thought of the whole family falling apart is overwhelming.

Just as alcoholism is passed on to the next generation if your dysfunctional family does not seek help, you will replicate the unhealthy family system when you have children of your own. The future generations will carry the burden of the damaging rules and customs of the preceding generations. This is how co-dependency is passed from one generation to the next.

The Disease Of Co-dependency

When you try to take care of unhealthy parents and protect your family system, you have no time to be a child. You are not allowed to have feelings and needs because they are too threatening. Your emotional growth becomes stunted. You learn to play your role, follow the rules and do what is expected of you. In your heart you feel you have to act this way to help your parents and family. You believe that if you truly love your family, you will keep trying to save it. As you continue to abandon yourself, you fall prey to the disease of co-dependency.

In time the behaviors you learn to survive and to try to save your family become permanent masks. You can lose touch with your true self. As Robert Subby notes, you invest more psychological energy into a *false self* than into your true self. When you live long enough with your false self, your co-dependency takes on a life of its own, even when you leave home. Because you do not develop your true self, Subby calls co-dependency "a delayed identity syndrome." (*Lost In The Shuffle*).

In her book, *Choicemaking,* Sharon Wegscheider-Cruse calls co-dependency . . .

"... a specific condition characterized by preoccupation and extreme dependence (emotionally, socially and sometimes physically) on a person or object. Eventually this dependence on another person becomes a pathological condition that affects the co-dependent in all other relationships."

Anne Wilson Schaef has identified this same pathological condition in our society as a whole. She looks at how a society can operate as a dysfunctional system, just as a family can.

The Addictive Process

The term *co-dependent* was first used to identify someone who was close to an alcoholic or chemically dependent person. Professionals in the alcohol and drug field began to see that the people around the alcoholic suffered as severely as the addicted person. Since then co-dependency (also referred to as co-dependence) has taken on a broader meaning. The term no longer applies only to someone who is affected by an addicted person.

Co-dependency now refers to people who are afflicted by their own addictive process. They may come from families in which there were no noticeable addictions. Everything may have looked fine on the surface, but the parents were emotionally unavailable to the children and to each other. And because addiction is built into our society most people, regardless of their family background, need to recover from some form of addictiveness.

The prefix *co* in the term co-dependency means to me *in relation to* an addictive process. If you are co-dependent, your addictive process leads you to be compulsively dependent in relation to anything. Your addictive process can come out in any number of ways. You can become addicted to substances, people, ideas, activities, behaviors or anything that takes away the pain of reality and gives you a sense of personal identity. The addictive process is the same regardless of the addiction.

Therefore, to free your heart and become fully alive it is necessary to heal on two levels: to arrest your addictions, as well as to heal your underlying disease of co-dependency.

You can attend 12-Step support groups and adopt specific behavior changes to free yourself from your addictions. The 12-Step support groups are modeled after Alcoholics Anonymous (see Appendix I). Alcoholics Anonymous addresses recovery from alcoholism. The 12-Step program, however, can also be used to recover from any addiction and to strengthen your spiritual connection in the world. There are many other 12-Step groups, such as Al-Anon, for people who are close to an addicted person; Adult Children of Alcoholics, for people from dysfunctional families; co-dependency support groups; Narcotics Anonymous, for drug dependency; Cocaine Anonymous; Overeaters Anonymous; Sex and Love Addicts Anonymous and more.

As you arrest your addictions, you can also work with a therapist who is knowledgeable about co-dependency. In therapy you can gradually heal the issues from your family of origin. You can grieve for the unconditional support you did not receive as a child and begin to bring your true self out into the world again. But without this deeper healing, you will be more likely to return to addictions when the repressed parts of yourself eventually surface.

As you heal on these two levels, they will work together to deepen your recovery. As you arrest your addictions, you will be more open to seeing the truth about your past and to feeling your long repressed feelings. And the more you work through your deepest grief, the less you will need to turn to addictions to escape reality.

As with any other disease, if you do not seek help your co-dependency will progress. As you fall prey to addictions and continually live from a false self, you will eventually break down under the strain. Untreated co-dependency invariably leads to stress-related complications, physical illness, depression and death. Fortunately, although it is a chronic and fatal disease, co-dependency is also treatable.

The disease of co-dependency is especially challenging to treat because it can be subtle and insidious. You may have a successful career and look all together on the outside, but feel tense and uneasy on the inside. This can make it difficult for you to seek help. You may not be able to make sense of the way you feel and you may not see a cause for your pain. Co-dependents often say, "Everything's fine in my life. I'm married, I've got a family and great kids. I should be happy, but I feel so empty."

It is important for you to understand that you are not at fault for having the disease of co-dependency: It was passed on to you whether you wanted it or not. As with any disease, your responsibility begins once you are aware of what can be done to treat your problem. At this point you can begin to recover your personal power and choose the kind of life you want.

Late Onset Co-dependency

It is possible to suffer from co-dependency even if your parents were not emotionally unavailable. If you come from a relatively healthy family but you stay with an untreated partner, you can get caught in the abuse cycle of a dysfunctional relationship. You can develop *late onset co-dependency*. This means if your partner is co-dependent and lives by dysfunctional rules, you can develop co-dependent symptoms as an adult.

If you develop co-dependency later in life it is probably an indication that you had the seeds of the disease within you before you entered into an unhealthy relationship. Becoming intimately involved with an unhealthy person can set off your latent co-dependency. If you grew up in a healthy family you can still be affected by the addictive messages in our media and in society at large. This can leave you vulnerable to developing some degree of co-dependency. If, on the other hand, you find a partner who was also raised in a healthy family, you may go through life relatively free of co-dependent traits.

The Symptoms Of Co-dependency

If you tried to help your parents with their problems when you were a young child, you have probably realized that your efforts were not successful. You were not able to pacify angry parents, make unhappy parents happy or stop alcoholic parents from drinking. No matter how hard you tried you could not save your parents and your family.

The futility of trying to solve the problems of your family affects you deeply. As a child you did not realize that you were not to blame for your parents' problems. As Middelton-Moz and Dwinell explain, you reacted to their pain out of innocence and helplessness:

> "A child is not able to discern that he or she is interacting with the illness of alcoholism or . . . co-dependency, rather than with a parent. Hence the child tends to internalize blame for all that goes wrong. . . . "

After the Tears

Taking on such responsibility as a child was very damaging to you. You began to believe that you had power to control other people. In fact, you believed that you needed to control others in order for you to be safe and to be loved.

In time you lost sight of the distinction between healthy concern for others and *caretaking*. When you caretake you try to do something for people that only they can do for themselves. You try to control what is beyond your limits. This is not human kindness, it is co-dependency. It is natural human behavior gone awry.

Some of the symptoms you may develop when you learn to caretake others are low self-esteem, a fear of abandonment, an urge to control yourself and others, delusion, weak personal boundaries, lack of trust, compulsive behaviors and obsessive thinking. You may be unaware of what you are feeling or have difficulty expressing your feelings. You can feel isolated even when you are with people. You may fear authority figures, feeling that you are a victim. And because you assume responsibility for the sickness of your family system, you judge yourself harshly for failing to save them.

If you are co-dependent, you may live with an underlying sense that something is wrong with you, that you are somehow incomplete and inadequate. You may feel that you are faking it in life and if people find out what you are really like, they will reject you.

When you grow up in a dysfunctional family, the past is still very much alive. Even if you are unaware of it, you face each day as if an alcoholic parent were around every corner, waiting to attack you. You project your past fears onto people in your life today. You may know that your fears are not appropriate in the present but your disease can be so strong, you become conditioned not to trust, to react in old ways.

As a child you may have witnessed and experienced acts of emotional, physical and sexual abuse. These may have been committed in the name of love and later rationalized as, "I did it for your own good." You probably grew up in a family in which there was not enough love to go around, where you had to bury your true self to care for others. When you cut off from your true self, you cut off from your intuitive sense of how to love. Without this inner knowledge to guide you, you live by illusions of what it means to love someone and how far you have to go to be considered a caring person.

Co-dependency Checklist

The following statements can help you identify co-dependent thinking. They reveal what many people mistake for love. See if any ring true for you.

1. I will be careful of what I say and do so that you will not get angry at me. All of my efforts must be aimed towards controlling you so that you will not reject me.
2. My feeling good about myself comes from being liked by you, by receiving approval from you, from *not* receiving criticism from you.
3. If you are unhappy, I am unhappy. If I can solve your problems and take away your pain, I will gain self-worth and you will appreciate me.
4. I do not know what I want and what I feel. I am only interested in you and your needs. My opinions, beliefs, dreams, hobbies, friends and interests are secondary to your life. The way you live is better than the way I live.
5. You can read my mind and know what I want. You will behave the way I want, without my having to tell you. We are a reflection of each other. I don't know where I leave off and you begin.

The World Of The Fragile

Co-dependents live in a world in which they often believe people are so fragile that you must do extraordinary things to help others cope with life. Life itself is perceived as fragile so people cannot be expected to take care of themselves. A "good" person must try to help others. This fragility calls for extraordinary protectiveness, patience and saintly compassion. However coarse, rude or overpowering a person's behavior, that person has a spirit that is suffering. That does not mean, however, that you must tolerate unacceptable behavior and treat such a person as you would a crystal in danger of shattering.

Human beings *are* fragile. Bodies can be easily damaged by disease, accidents and wars. Hearts can be broken, minds wasted.

Excessive fragility can be used as a rationalization for manipulative behavior and self-delusion. The next time you are afraid to go against someone's wishes because of his or her fragility, just remember: *you* are fragile, too. People can be a lot stronger than they seem. And they need to go through painful emotions to grow and mature. You actually may not be helping by focusing only on a person's vulnerability.

The Slightest Mistake

Given that people are perceived as so fragile, so needy, so unable to cope and you consider yourself responsible for them, you believe that the slightest mistake can cause pain and disaster. You live with a self-imposed obligation to strive relentlessly for perfection. You may pay lip service to the idea that we are all just human, but you are driven by internal messages that tell you that you are a bad person if you aren't perfect.

You may tell yourself something similar to what Don said,

"Life's not fair, but a good person doesn't try to weasel out of responsibility, doesn't whine about it. He accepts that people are vulnerable, that little mistakes and human imperfections can damage lives and souls. He learns to live with this reality."

The Final Straw

When you believe people are so fragile you must spare them the slightest problem, you can fall for another myth: that any emotional demand you make upon others may be the "final straw" that breaks their back, making you responsible for destroying them.

This "final straw" is a bizarre responsibility to assume. A person is under stress or in trouble because of many cumulative factors to which you may have contributed nothing or very little. Yet you assume it is your behavior that pushes him or her over the edge. Accepting this undeserved guilt allows you to be manipulated easily because you feel you are at fault whenever people are upset.

Jim took the "final straw" myth to its logical conclusion. He always seemed to bump into people just when his needs were the "final straw" that overwhelmed the person. He felt cursed. It seemed there was nothing he could do, no one he could get involved with who he wouldn't ruin.

The last straw that led Jim to seek treatment for this excessive sense of responsibility was an incident with his friend Pete. Pete had been depressed for months and rejected Jim's many offers of help and support. One day Pete was telling Jim how awful his life was and Jim dared to say how frustrated he was with Pete's refusal to seek professional help. Two days later, Pete attempted suicide with pills and alcohol. Jim felt it was somehow his fault and suffered tremendous guilt. "If only," he thought, "I had not become angry with Pete, maybe this wouldn't have happened."

This inappropriate sense of power over another caused Jim enough pain to seek treatment for himself. Through treatment, Jim realized he was not responsible for Pete's behavior. He saw that he had enabled his friend by not setting personal boundaries. It would have been healthier for Jim to say, "It is too painful for me to see you in this condition. Either you get professional help along with talking with me, or I have to back off for my own health."

Conflict Ahead — Look Out!

Another myth co-dependents live by is that conflict hurts people and needs to be avoided at all costs. You may have noticed when conflict arises how quickly many people turn their attention from the content of the disagreement to the way in which you are conversing. People who have no positive experience in resolving conflicts tend to make the issue one of blame, rather than facing the issues that caused the argument.

Leslie remembers when she got angry as a child, her mother would not address Leslie's concerns. Instead, her mother would cry, "I can't take it. I can't take your criticism. I can't take your yelling at me."

Leslie learned that conflicts were considered bad. In her family disagreements threatened her parents' artificial state of emotional stability and control. If she challenged this, she robbed them of something they apparently needed to survive emotionally.

There are many things co-dependents do to avoid even an implied conflict with people and to maintain the illusion of closeness and intimacy. Ask yourself if you have made any of these behaviors part of your life:

- Have you ever avoided confronting people when they hurt your feelings?
- Have you ever stopped yourself from getting angry or showing anger so that people do not have to feel badly about their behavior?
- Do you pass over what someone says or let him or her think you feel the same way, when actually you disagree or feel quite differently?
- Do you pretend everything is okay when it's not?
- Have you ever taken abuse and put-downs and swallowed your feelings instead of standing up for yourself?
- Do you let something go by instead of asking for clarification — blaming yourself when others are inconsistent? "I must have misunderstood," you tell yourself.
- Do you ever ignore your own basic needs for comfort or support, or downplay your accomplishments so that you don't challenge the priority of someone else's needs over your own?
- Did you ever do something for someone because you were afraid that if you didn't, he or she would go off the deep end or wouldn't like you anymore?

- Have you ever felt guilty because you couldn't get your parent to stop drinking, or because you couldn't get your spouse to be a "good" spouse?
- Have you ever felt guilty for saying what you don't like about someone's behavior because that person is so nice?

If you are co-dependent, you may be able to identify with several of these behaviors. As you grow in recovery, you will become more comfortable with healthy disagreements.

One way to avoid conflict is to be "nice." *Perpetual niceness* is a compulsive defensive behavior. It is hard to communicate with someone who maintains such an image. As you learn to trust your intuition, you can tell when someone is using niceness abusively. When they do, you may feel a little off-center or even feel a person has taken advantage of you. Genuine thoughtfulness feels quite different. It has a clear full quality to it, as if someone is unconditionally regarding you, instead of trying to slip by.

Al was "the nicest person you ever wanted to meet." Whenever someone asked him to do something, he would agree to do it. Sometimes he would actually do it, but often he would not. He was so nice about it, however, that it was difficult to confront him when he failed to keep his word. If someone confronted him, he always had an apology and an excuse. He would never be held accountable for his behavior.

Another way in which co-dependents avoid conflict is by saying, "I can't," when what they really mean is "I won't" or "I don't want to." If there is potential for conflict, it can feel too threatening to say, "I don't want to" — to take responsibility for refusing to do something. "I can't" allows you to remain in a victim's role. If forced out of this role, you would have to confront the reason why a direct refusal is so threatening. You would have to take the risk to put your needs out front and to set a limit, which to a co-dependent means you would be bad and the other person wouldn't love you anymore.

Jeff had never learned to clearly state his limitations. Whenever someone made a demand on him that he did not want to meet, he would start explaining why he could not do it, rather than standing his ground, negotiating or politely refusing. When one of his more dominating friends did not let Jeff get away with "I can't," Jeff could no longer avoid taking responsibility for his decisions. Jeff ended up desperately defending his refusal, actually pleading with his friend to believe him that it was not his choice, but that he really was powerless to do what his friend wanted.

"I'm not trying to give you a hard time," Jeff would plead. "Believe me, I'd do it if I could. I'm really sorry. I don't want to disappoint you."

What Jeff needed to learn is that "no" is a complete sentence. Avoiding a confrontation does not resolve a conflict, it only buries and postpones it. There are clear and tactful ways in which you can address issues and take responsibility for yourself.

The Self-Image Of The Caretaker

You are probably not conscious of the many ways in which you can give other people's needs priority over your own. These behaviors become automatic. You may misinterpret your actions, as Jeff did, and think you are doing something to avoid causing someone else suffering, when you are actually avoiding your own fear of abandonment.

Co-dependents build their lives around caretaking for others. They may even acknowledge their purpose in life is to protect another person's feelings. The reason given? To expiate an unending sense of guilt, to salvage a life that otherwise would be meaningless or to avoid being selfish. If you think this way, you may even get angry at yourself for having needs.

Carla, for example, felt that caretaking was all she was fit to do, considering how inadequate and defective she felt.

"I felt very strongly," she said, "that there was no point in my trying to pick a career I really wanted or do anything exciting for myself. From an early age I felt it was wrong to have a life of my own, with goals and dreams of my own. I didn't deserve it. I was too crazy and caused too much suffering. The only thing to do then was to make the best of a bad business and help others."

Carla was subject to deep depressions in which she felt she had no right to live and should kill herself. In such moments of despair, if she could remember a good deed she had done recently — such as letting a rude person barge in front of her to get on a bus in the pouring rain — then she allowed herself another temporary lease on life.

Beware of taking on the role of lifelong caretaker of other people's feelings. This pattern can become so ingrained that it is a shock and an agony to let it go, to accept that most people do not need to be taken care of in this way. Healthy people enjoy you and get energy from you when you like yourself and do your own things — when you take care of *yourself*. Co-dependency is the antithesis of self-care. It is putting your focus on people, places and things outside of yourself, instead of first checking in with yourself and coming from an inner place. But there is a wonderful paradox. By "selfishly" enjoying your own growth, happiness and inner strength, you give to others. That is to say, people who really love you and are healthy will enjoy seeing you happily going about your life. And when you take care of yourself and give to others, you will do so from a full heart, instead of from a position of depletion.

Eleanor Roosevelt once said, "When you cease to make a contribution, you begin to die." Let your contribution be one of health and love, not co-dependent caretaking. Treating someone as a person, honoring another person's being with your full presence, and developing your ability to have empathy for yourself and others, are all appropriate contributions of love and kindness.

The Ties That Bind

As we have seen, family systems operate in accordance with certain accepted family rules, customs and expectations. When a family is dysfunctional, these guidelines become rigid and harmful to the family members. We will look in detail at the restrictions that hold together a dysfunctional family system. We will look at *invisible loyalties, shameful family secrets, enmeshment, dysfunctional family rules,* and *family roles.* All of these ensure that you take care of the unhealthy family system at the expense of your individual health and spirit. Instead of being healthy guidelines for living in a family, they teach you how to be co-dependent and shroud your genuine loving spirit.

Loyal To The End

Families create and transmit invisible loyalties. According to sociologist Ivan Boszormenyi-Nagy, in every family there exists strong but not easily discernible pressures to respond to the demands for fairness among members of the family. If someone has been hurt or suffered a disappointment or loss, then someone else may be expected to make a sacrifice or go out of his or her way to make compensation.

This can be a healthy process because reciprocal acts help create a feeling of fairness in a family. For instance, it is important to give back to those who have given you so much, as in the case of parents and children. Your parents gave you the most basic gift, that of life. It is natural for you to want to give them something in return. It is also healthy to make up for your past negative behavior with positive actions in the present. If you do not do this you may feel extremely guilty.

Every family has traditions it attempts to instill in each new generation. Many times these traditions are a code of "family honor" that passes on a message of decent behavior, moral integrity and personal independence. Children can make their families proud by making the most of their lives, succeeding in the world in some way and turning out to be decent caring loving human beings.

Parents can pass on folk wisdom in the form of "old saws" and sayings. As you get older you may find yourself saying, "My dad always used to say . . ." — and you may be surprised that your parents knew a thing or two. Children are also influenced by traditions from various cultures that have swept through America in waves of immigration. These have brought us loyalties and expectations related to religion, patriotism, social class and sex roles that have become bound up in family dynamics.

Sometimes these loyalties can be carried too far. Instead of general guidelines to help you cope with life, they become rigid specific expectations. As an adult you carry these loyalties with you as unconscious urges to behave in the same ways as your parents, even when these behaviors are detrimental.

Sometimes the expectations are so rigid they leave no room for you to explore and develop your individuality. For instance, a woman may hate men, just as her mother did. Or a son may act superior to women to stay loyal to his father. These kinds of loyalties can be particularly damaging because they can be deeply rooted in the unconscious. When parents have rigid expectations of you and have overinvested emotion and identity in these expectations, you may feel a need to take care of your parents by not disappointing their expectations.

An unconscious loyalty could be a compulsion to make up for a parent's failures or for wrongs (real or imagined) committed against the family. It may be a need to address issues that were not resolved in previous generations. You may try to make up for the loss of a sibling. You may restrict your activities at school for fear that your parents would not approve.

For instance, you may not join the glee club if your parents do not want you to perform in front of people. You may excel in athletics because you know your father was a star athlete but injured himself and was unable to achieve his goals in sports. The following stories illustrate the power of invisible loyalties.

Doug

Doug was 34 years old and worked 80 hours a week as an investor for his alcoholic father. He tried to get his father's approval by putting together million-dollar deals. When Doug succeeded, his father scarcely acknowledged Doug's achievement. Doug had no life of his own. He had unconsciously dedicated his life to his father and had made his father his Higher Power.

Doug finally sought help because his life was in such turmoil. He was turning to a number of prescription drugs to alleviate his emotional pain, as well as his progressively accumulative physical problems. In therapy Doug realized he was carrying his father's shame so his father would not have to face his own problems. By feeling sorry for his father and taking on his father's feelings, Doug was caught in *enmeshed empathy*. His natural concern for his father had grown out of proportion.

With the help of his therapist and co-dependency inpatient treatment, Doug was able to let his father choose the life he wanted. Doug began to let go of his father and feel his own grief at not receiving the love and attention he needed. Doug began to take responsibility for his life. He realized by taking care of his father's pain, he had been making it harder for his father to seek help. Often a person's pain can be a motivation to find recovery.

Marilyn

Marilyn was an extremely intelligent woman who worked as a waitress. She wanted to go to college but could not bring herself to do it. Her family was poor and she had always been reminded by her parents of their low economic and social status. This became Marilyn's identity. She had an invisible loyalty to stay poor, even though she had the intelligence to go to college and pursue a career. Once Marilyn brought this loyalty to the surface, she made a conscious choice to let go of the idea of perpetual poverty. She enrolled in college and studied to become a certified public accountant. Whenever her family loyalty would start to creep back into her mind and she began to feel guilty for wanting a career, she would affirm to herself, "Marilyn, you can be more successful than your parents. It's okay. You can be a success and still be a lovable person."

The issue of loyalty is a delicate one in the family. The breaking of family loyalties can lead to family conflicts and upset the family equilibrium. You need to be able to express feelings and thoughts that conflict with others in the family in order to mature and to become an individual. However, as Boszormenyi-Nagy and Spark point out, in a dysfunctional family . . . "every move toward maturation represents an implicit threat of disloyalty to the system." *(Invisible Loyalties)*

In other words, your personal growth and normal identity development may be taken as a betrayal of your family. This can be very damaging to you. You may know that you need to go against your family at times to be true to yourself, but feel guilty and angry when your family meets your efforts with resistance. You may wonder why your family does not encourage you to follow your heart, when they claim to love you unconditionally. You may want to resist your family's pressure to conform but be confused about how far to go in caring for yourself.

It is unhealthy when loyalty to a past way of thinking or acting causes you to sacrifice your present life. An obsessive loyalty can also bring about personal problems because it encourages feelings of paranoia and a sense of being victimized. The family can adopt a mentality of "us against them" and barricade itself against the world. This undermines your ability to function confidently in society when it is time to leave home.

Because loyalties to the past are largely unconscious, it may be difficult for you to see how they affect you in the present day. You may want to ask yourself what kind of expectations create a crisis of loyalty in your family. For instance:

- Do you feel pressure to live near your parents and raise your children according to their ideas?
- Do you owe it to your parents to have grandchildren?
- How much time must you spend with your family?
- How much do you have to do to make your parents feel loved?
- Do you have to become a doctor to please your father?
- Do you have to become an engineer because it is a profession that runs in your family?
- If you are a woman, did you give up having a social life to have a career which would make your father proud of you?
- Do you have to become a supermom to gain your parents' approval?

The most basic questions may be these: What do you deserve as a child? What do your parents owe you? How much gratitude do you need to show your parents? Asking yourself these questions can help you to uncover the invisible loyalties in your life.

Shameful Secrets

Co-dependency is a shame-based disease. As John Bradshaw notes in his book, *Healing The Shame That Binds You*, shame is . . . "a healthy human power which can become a true sickness of the soul."

Shame becomes destructive when it is passed down through the generations. Children in a dysfunctional home carry the shame, as well as the anger, pain and fear, that was never confronted in an appropriate way by their parents and grandparents. Their healthy feelings of shame, anger, fear and pain are buried by the burden of past generations of unacknowledged emotions. Healthy shame is a feeling of mild embarrassment that helps you to be accountable for your actions. *Carried shame*, or *toxic shame*, is an overwhelming emotion passed on to you from your parents. It makes you feel small and unworthy and, as Pia Mellody describes in her book *Facing Co-dependence*, "less than" everyone else. This kind of shame can lead you to deny your feelings. You can also act shamelessly and abuse others to make up for your feelings of inadequacy by feeling "more than" others.

Toxic shame is not the same as guilt. You may feel guilty in regard to a specific action. You can acknowledge that your behavior was inappropriate or harmful, if that is in fact true, and you can change your behavior. When you feel toxic shame, you feel there is nothing you can do about it. You're inherently wrong.

One way that shame is passed on to the children in a dysfunctional family is through shameful secrets. The secret could be anything from the disease of alcoholism to financial irresponsibility. Many children feel a need to vindicate parents who did things that embarrassed them, or rehabilitate a painful image of their parents. It could be a child's guilty secret, such as masturbation, or a "shameful" family member who was illegitimate or retarded. It may be something specific such as incest or something as general as hiding the reality that the family is not ideal and does not live up to the standards of society. When conformity is king, children can be ashamed of anything that makes their family different. Your loyalty out of shame can be very strong and can reinforce your urge to take care of your dysfunctional family system.

Stuck Like Glue

In dysfunctional families, emotional needs are not fulfilled and conflicts are seldom resolved. This results in a stickiness that Murray Bowen calls *enmeshment*. In an enmeshed family, when you try to change the way you relate to others it sets off a chain of events that serve to keep things the way they are. To preserve the family system, family members intrude upon each other and violate each other's personal thoughts, feelings and activities. There is little room for autonomy or privacy. Generational boundaries are weak and easily crossed, resulting in role confusion (Murray Bowen, 1976).

Enmeshment allows family members to maintain their defenses against their fear of intimacy and pain. They want you to take care of them by joining them in preserving all of the toxic patterns in the family that block the expression of feelings. This is why caring can become so twisted in a dysfunctional family. When you play caretaker of people's defenses, you support their misery in addictions and co-dependency. When you try to address their real needs you appear to attack their defenses, upon which they depend for survival, and you can be accused of disloyalty, cruelty, indifference and selfishness.

Enmeshment is a sticky feeling, a "trapped in glue" feeling, as if when you try to be yourself, you feel a giant rubber band pulling you back to the family. It is a feeling of addiction. Old patterns are familiar, no matter how self-destructive, and breaking away from them is accompanied by feelings of panic, disorientation, a guilty feeling that you are doing something wrong — in short, withdrawal.

Enmeshment leads to the social isolation of the family. Parents tend to make few friends outside the family, therefore, each family member must get all his or her needs fulfilled by the family. Often these needs are not stated directly or clearly so go unacknowledged. Family members are somehow expected to "read minds" — to know what others need, to fulfill these needs or face anger, resentment or accusations of betrayal. This expectation of mind-reading is learned. You may find yourself doing it as an adult — angry when a friend or spouse does not do something you expected of him or her without being asked. "She should have known," you may think. "If he really loved me, he would have seen . . . "

A Sense Of Your Self

Murray Bowen's concept of *differentiation of self* can help you to understand how enmeshment affects you and keeps you from living from your true self. Differentiation of self refers to your ability to distinguish between thinking clearly for yourself and thinking in ways distorted by your emotions. In a dysfunctional family system, it is virtually impossible for you as a child to respond rationally to events. The longer you are in the dysfunction, the more you will react automatically, driven by unresolved feelings such as guilt, fear and abandonment. As a result, you do not develop a separate identity with clear beliefs and principles. You become a prisoner of your own overwhelming emotions. As an adult you tend to be attracted to people like yourself who do not have clear personal boundaries and distinct identities, and you pass these traits on to your children.

Bowen has developed a scale to measure the degree to which your intellect and emotions guide your behavior. This scale can help you see the strength of your codependency — the ways in which you may still look to other people and external things to give you a sense of self-worth.

On Bowen's scale, 0-25 means low self-differentiation; 25-50 means moderate self-differentiation; 50-75 means moderate-to-good self-differentiation; and 75-100 is left open as an ideal.

Here are profiles of each level based on Bowen's work. As you read these, take a deep breath. You may find that they affect you deeply, for Bowen's categories embody our struggles to escape dysfunctional systems and find our own light.

Low Self-Differentiation

According to Bowen, the lower level of the scale shows *fusion* which in its simplest form can be defined as the domination of one family member by another. In relation to the family system, fusion means a state in which a person is almost wholly dependent on the feelings of those around him or her. This dependency is aptly described by Bowen's term *undifferentiated family ego mass*, which

means a quality of emotional oneness or "stuck together-
ness" in a family system.

If you have severe problems with addiction or co-
dependency, you have a low level of self-differentiation.
You live in a feeling-dominated world. This does not
mean you process feelings in a healthy flowing way. It
means that overwhelming feelings confuse your sense
of reality.

Sam, for example, knew that his wife Rita didn't like to
go to the opera because she did not care for opera, not
because she did not want to be with Sam. Sometimes Rita
would go with Sam, but most of the time she declined.
Sam could not shake the feeling of being rejected. Often
when Rita did not want to see an opera, Sam would end
up accusing Rita of not loving him. He simply could not
distinguish his feelings from facts.

Another earmark of low self-differentiation is being
obsessively relationship-oriented to the exclusion of much
else. So much of your energy goes into seeking love and
approval and keeping your relationships in some kind of
harmony, you have little energy for other life-directed
goals. Your life can become a day-to-day struggle to keep
a relationship in balance or to achieve some degree of
comfort and freedom from anxiety. Without constant support, you do not feel you can make it.

When you do not have a strong sense of yourself, your
confidence can become so low you feel false and insecure
whenever you express an opinion. Making long-term
goals becomes impossible, except as vague generalities
such as, "I want to be successful."

One of Sam's clues to the state of low self-differentiation in his family was that his parents often told him, "I
want you to be happy," but their actions thwarted all his
efforts to establish his own life.

According to Bowen, people with low self-differentiation are, "vulnerable to stress, life adjustments are more

difficult and they have a high incidence of human illness and problems." (*Family Therapy in Clinical Practice*)

At this level if you do not seek help, your ability to function can deteriorate. You become caught in a vicious cycle of acting rashly on your emotions or being immobilized by them, rather than thinking the situation through. This leads to greater dysfunction in your life and heightened anxiety, which further paralyzes you or triggers more actions based solely on emotions and the cycle continues.

Moderate Self-Differentiation

If your self-differentiation is at a moderate level you are likely to have a better understanding of the interplay between thought and emotion. You are still very concerned with winning friends and worrying about what others think. Although you express your feelings more openly, you still depend on others to build your self-esteem. Your confidence can soar with a compliment or be crushed by criticism. Success still means pleasing others or controlling a relationship.

Some of these patterns may seem very familiar to you because this level of emotional dependency on others is frequently reflected in our culture and arts. For instance, popular movies and novels tend to idealize love and portray quests for the "perfect" relationship. If you are at a level of moderate self-differentiation, it seems natural to be hypersensitive to the moods, expressions and postures of others. You may tend to react impulsively, often expressing feelings that are inappropriate for the situation.

Another familiar pattern is to run from one relationship to another. Often you pursue excessive and instant closeness, which leads to fusion. But when the person gets too close, you withdraw, which stimulates another fusion cycle.

At this level of self-differentiation, you still have a hard time standing up for yourself or expressing your beliefs. You may rely too heavily on citing authorities, rather than having confidence in your own judgment. You may be a bit of a chameleon, tending to agree with anyone you talk to, afraid to provoke conflict or risk disapproval. You may fall compulsively into the role of the disciple or try to maintain your sense of self by being a rebel, fighting and debating with everything other people say, especially authority figures. You may never give yourself a chance to sort through what you really think.

When your self-differentiation is moderate, you probably feel more comfortable with knowledge about impersonal things than with insights into your emotions and relationships. With little faith in yourself when it comes to personal matters, your personal life tends to be in chaos. You fear your emotions and try to block them. You may appear intellectually oriented or aloof on the surface, but your rigid control is a defense. Inside your emotions boil wildly and you do not know how to let them out or experience them in a healthy way.

Your sense of yourself can depend greatly on your level of anxiety. When your anxiety is low, your functioning can resemble good levels of self-differentiation. When your anxiety is high, your functioning can resemble that of low levels of self-differentiation. At this stage it is best to avoid *toxic people* — those whose negativity or dysfunction tends to bring on the type of anxiety that undermines self-worth and makes it difficult to function or feel good about yourself. It is also best to avoid the temptation to turn to an addiction to relieve the anxiety of the moment.

Moderate-To-Good Self-Differentiation

Having good self-differentiation means that your mind and emotions can function as a cooperative team. You are no longer a victim of your emotions. You are able to live freely and have a more satisfying emotional life. Your instincts and intuition can guide you effectively most of the time. In critical situations, you have the discipline to overrule your emotional reactions and to think things through. This is not the same as using your intellect as a defense against feeling. It does not mean that you are a rigid, nonfeeling person. It means that you do not have to be dominated by anxiety. You can sometimes run on auto-pilot but when trouble develops, you can take over, calm the anxiety, think clearly and avoid a crisis. This is what we mean by trusting life and trusting yourself.

If your self-differentiation is good, you are able to follow independent life goals. You are aware of the impor-tance of relationships but are able to determine your life course more from within than from what others think. You are able to have healthy relationships with your par-ents, friends and lovers. Balance, compromise and give and take become possible when you honor your feelings, but are not controlled by them.

You are also better able to state your convictions calmly, without attacking the beliefs of others and without feeling you have to defend everything you say. Differences are respected. There is room for more than one opinion. You do not feel an overwhelming need to overvalue or under-value yourself in relation to others. You do not blame others for failures or credit anyone else for your successes.

Moving Toward The Ideal

On the path of freedom from addictions and recovery from co-dependency, you can move into the high self-differentiation level. At this level you are able to sustain ambiguity and be open to all possibilities. You feel strong enough and big enough to contain all of your emotions. You neither have to discharge them nor repress them. You can just be with them and learn what they have to teach you. Then you can choose how and when to express them, if, indeed, you wish to.

You move toward the ideal when you recover from the shameful sense of feeling less than others and from the need to feel greater than others. You can feel as though you are an equal unique valuable person. It is a sign of the disease to think that you are better or worse than someone else. It is a spiritual offense to yourself and to others. With high self-differentiation your thinking is clear enough to perceive and accept that every human being is precious.

Dysfunctional Family Rules

In an unhealthy family system oppressive loyalties inhibit normal growth, shameful secrets must be hidden and family members become enmeshed in unresolved emotional tensions. These patterns are passed on from generation to generation. One of the most powerful ways in which this happens is that parents consciously or unconsciously teach their children to rigidly follow dysfunctional family rules. In a sense these unhealthy rules are how you learn to be co-dependent.

Claudia Black identifies three basic rules: *Don't Talk, Don't Trust,* and *Don't Feel.*

In his book, *Lost In The Shuffle,* Robert Subby looks at several of the following family rules. Although every family develops its own variations, these rules are universal in one form or another in dysfunctional families. See how many of the rules strike a responsive chord in you. Even if you have never put them into words, you have probably learned them and lived by them for too long.

1. Don't trust.
2. Don't feel and if you do, don't let anyone know what you're feeling.
3. Don't talk: Keep quiet, don't bring up problems, don't mention sex and money.
4. Don't breathe — don't exist.
5. Don't know what you know, and certainly don't say what you know.
6. Always know what you're doing and where you're going.
7. Be strong and always in control.
8. Never need help but if you do, don't ask for it.
9. Don't play or be childlike.
10. Do as I say, not as I do.
11. Do the right thing (never clearly defined).
12. Be good (as if you're bad and must become good).

13. Don't rock the boat.
14. Communicate only indirectly, using someone or something as a go-between or buffer (this is called *triangulation*).

These rules deny you the inner freedom to be yourself. They force you to grow up in a hurried fashion or at the other extreme, to never grow up. As a result of these rules, you may be determined to do things alone and find asking for help very difficult. You become accustomed to a rigidity that undermines trust and prevents intimacy. The child within you, who must be reached for true recovery, is repressed by patterns of extreme, distorted thinking and many forms of denial, such as, "Oh, every family has problems" and, "It wasn't that bad."

As John Bradshaw says,

> "(The rules) that unhealthy family systems live by . . . are based on an inequality of power and unequal rights. They promote the use and ownership of some people by others and teach the denial and repression of emotional vitality and spontaneity. They glorify obedience, orderliness, logic, rationality, power and male supremacy. They are flagrantly anti-life."
>
> *Bradshaw On: The Family*

The effect of these rules is so powerful that Robert Subby defines co-dependency as,

> ". . . an emotional, psychological or behavioral pattern of coping which develops as a result of prolonged exposure to and practice of a dysfunctional set of family rules. In turn these rules make difficult or impossible the open expression of thoughts and feelings. Normal identity development is thereby interrupted. It is the denial or repression of the real self."
>
> *Lost In The Shuffle*

Although family rules can suppress the growth of your inner being when they become rigid, they can be both healthy and unhealthy. You may be able to recall your family rules.

For example, in my family my father often took me aside and said, "When I make up my mind to do something, I do it." This attitude, that he had learned from his father and grandfather, struck me as a maxim of determination. In that light it was a family tradition that encouraged me to do my best in my career and personal endeavors. It encouraged me to have goals and the confidence that I could reach them. However, I tended to get caught in self-will, sometimes pursuing goals that were not in my best interest or stubbornly staying on a course after I realized it was not good for me.

The rule could also be used as an edict of unhealthy self-reliance. It could be an unconscious order to never ask for help, to never admit I was in trouble, overwhelmed or confronted with a situation I couldn't handle myself. And indeed, when I suspected I was in over my head, I would not ask for help but would force myself to work harder and, of course, deny that I was having any trouble. This family rule could make intellect into a god at the expense of intuition and emotion. I've had to learn not only to ask for help when appropriate, but also to let go of rigid thinking, to let my intuition guide me to be in touch with my gut feelings. Now when my thinking is in line with my feelings, my life flows in positive ways.

These family rules served another purpose: to take care of the family system and to assert that the family, despite its share of problems, should be able to handle everything itself without help or treatment. The rules, therefore, kept the family in co-dependent patterns. Later, under the influence of these rules, I stayed in a dysfunctional marriage because I was programmed not to give up. I thought that if I just tried harder, everything would be all right. That, of course, did not work and only perpetuated the problems.

Prison Of Silence

Katie was brought up in a family in which there was no alcoholism, but severe dysfunction and very rigid rules against talking about emotions. Everything had to be proper. Everything was always "fine." No one talked about feelings except that, once in a while, someone would let out a sharp cutting remark. Katie felt this revealed that under the surface her family was a cauldron of hostility with a pretty lid on it. Katie doubted her perceptions of her family's hostility because it was so well hidden. She was living in what seemed to be an emotional vacuum of niceness, a *prison of silence.*

When she married, she and her husband seemed to have the "perfect marriage." They had gone to the right schools, had the right jobs and their children were "perfect." But there was no emotional sharing whatsoever in the marriage. When she tried to reach out, to share her thoughts and feelings, her husband was completely unresponsive. He had no interest in sharing his inner experience. Once again, Katie found herself in a family situation controlled by dysfunctional rules. Everything seemed fine. A part of her sensed an underlying hostility, but she doubted her perceptions as she had done in her family of origin. Eventually, she realized that she was living in another prison of silence.

The rules in your family can control the most subtle aspects of your behavior. When you suppress your emotions, you can fall into patterns that restrict the way you breathe, the way you touch others and the way you relate to the physical sensations and aliveness of your body. I have found in working with body techniques, such as *Trager®* and *Mentastics®*, that suppressed anger and pain can appear as tensions in various parts of the body. The release of your body from its tensions often reveals a history of adaptations and suppressions, such as cringing, holding breath, clenching teeth and other physical defenses against the pain of living by unhealthy family rules.

Family Roles

Members of a family play various roles. In a healthy family one child may make more jokes at the dinner table than her siblings. Another child may tend to be more serious. These roles are not rigid, however. The more serious child will still feel free to let out a one-liner occasionally. And, when the more playful sibling comes home after a difficult experience at school, her concerns are taken very seriously by the family. Each child is honored as an individual first. The roles they play are secondary.

In a dysfunctional family system these roles become so rigid, they eventually make up an important part of an individual's identity. The most familiar roles among the children in an unhealthy family are the Family Hero, the Lost Child, the Scapegoat, and the Mascot (Wegscheider-Cruse, 1981).

The Family Hero is often the oldest child. He or she is the super-responsible child. If you assume this role, you become a little parent. As far as you can tell, your parents are unable to run the family. Your fear that the family will fall apart is so strong, you do all you can to fill in for your parents.

Sophie's parents were both alcoholic. They would drink at night and on the weekends, letting the house fall into disrepair. When Sophie was eight years old, she learned how to cook, clean and iron. She would get up before her parents, make breakfast for her younger sisters and walk them to school. She told me, "I figured somebody had to take care of my sisters and clean the house, so I did it. I was too embarrassed to have anyone see our house when it was such a mess. I grew up fast."

The Lost Child responds to the dysfunctional family by becoming invisible. As a Lost Child you believe that the less you bother your parents, the better. You know they already have more than they can handle, so you are careful not to put demands on anyone. Often this child can be found spending hours alone, playing with dolls or trucks or reading books.

The Scapegoat is the child who constantly gets into trouble. By acting out, the Scapegoat distracts the family from its problems. This is the child who has a reputation for causing trouble. If a child gets blamed often enough, he or she will expect to be punished and behave accordingly.

Another role is the *Mascot* or the family clown. This child uses humor as a defense against the troubles in the family, and will usually be the initiator of the family's jokes, as well as the target. The Mascot learns to make friends by keeping people entertained.

Although each child learns to perform a role flawlessly, he or she can change roles when necessary. For instance, Seth was the Mascot in his family. Both of his parents had been raised in alcoholic homes and had not sought help for their co-dependency. Their marriage was tense and they rarely expressed their feelings. When Seth felt the tension between his parents at the dinner table, he would tell amusing stories to distract them. By drawing attention to himself, Seth was often able to interrupt their arguments.

Eventually Seth's parents got a divorce. Seth lived with his co-dependent mother and began to feel withdrawn and insecure. He stopped making jokes and became shy with the people he used to amuse so easily. Seth sought recovery for himself when he left home. He realized he had taken on the role of the Lost Child because he no longer needed his humor to try to pacify his parents. After working on his childhood issues, Seth was able to draw upon his natural gift for humor, but he no longer used it as a defense. He freed himself from both roles he had played and was able to live from his true self.

Children can also change roles when a sibling leaves home and his or her role needs to be filled. Whatever role you assume, your primary focus is on taking care of your dysfunctional family. The roles are simply another creative way in which you learn to survive. As with any survival skill, by closing your heart off from the pain around you, you further bury your inner spirit.

Love Never Dies

Co-dependent problems are rarely clearly defined. You may be healthy and functional in one area of your life and sick in another. Problems may be hidden when things are smooth, then erupt when you are under stress. Remember, if a problem interferes with your life and causes you pain, you need to think of yourself and take care of yourself. Even if a problem seems minor, it should be addressed or you run the risk of passing it on and making your children take care of you.

As you learn to distinguish between healthy and unhealthy behaviors and attitudes, you can start the process of recognizing your Inner Child and your deepest needs. You can re-experience caring in healthy ways and reclaim it for yourself from a position of inner strength. Through your recovery, you can bring love into all areas of your life.

Some Things To Do:
"How I Take Care Of My Parents"

If you'd like, take a minute to be alone. Go inside yourself and think back to your childhood. This may be scary to do, so be gentle with yourself. Be sure to breathe steadily and deeply.

Try to remember the way you were in your family system. If you can bring to mind visual images, that may help you. Ask yourself, "How did I usually behave? What was my role in the family? How did I act towards my parents?"

Think of ways in which you may have taken care of your parents. Did you try to guess what they wanted and act accordingly? Were you able to play as a child, or were you too busy worrying about your parents and your family? Did you give up activities that interested you or shun friends because you thought your parents wouldn't approve?

Write down anything that comes to you. If you're not sure whether certain behaviors were healthy, listen to your intuition. It may be able to give you a sense of when you were putting your parents' needs before your own.

Next, try looking at your values and the choices you have made as an adult. Ask yourself if you have continued to take care of your parents by staying loyal to them. Have you lived up to their expectations which may not be in line with what you really want? Look at your job, your relationships, your view of religion, your economic status, where you live, whether you have children and other areas of your life.

See if you can get a sense of where you still try to please your parents. Remember, the purpose of this is not to judge yourself, but to learn more about yourself so that you can be free to live from your true self.

PART
II

Caring At Different Ages

2

Cradle Robbers

What were you like as a young child?

For anyone from a dysfunctional family system, this can be a difficult question to answer. Think back and see what you can remember. You and I and all of us who have suffered traumatic childhoods will more than likely begin with repressed, distorted memories of our early years. Events may be forgotten or only vaguely recalled. You may realize your memory is filled with a series of emotional, familial or financial crises that overwhelm and blot out all else that happened. "I don't really recall very much of my years in grade school," you might say. "I was too busy dealing with my father's drinking and his abuse of my mother."

You might recall only a drama about yourself. One of my clients, Paul, told me he had an autobiography he could recite on command: the story of his battle to free himself from the influence of his domineering father. All other memories, good and bad, seemed unimportant and

45

were pale shadows compared with the vivid confrontations, betrayals and victories of his struggle for emotional independence.

You may be a person who when asked about your childhood, answers quickly and emotionlessly, "It wasn't that bad." Then you may sweep into your unconscious an array of heavily charged emotional associations. It wasn't that bad — the neglect, the void, the sarcasm, the beatings, the terror, the loneliness, the incestuous advances . . . it wasn't that bad. This is one of the most common ways in which co-dependents deny the terror and pain they experienced as children.

There may be those of you who don't remember much at all about your childhood, or those who say you were happy as far as you know. Others may say nothing much happened one way or the other. However you recall your childhood, it is very likely that there is something missing from your memories, something that is essential to your life and your spirit. Without these missing pieces, you will have a hard time understanding how to be a loving, compassionate person in ways that are not destructive to you and to people in your life.

It is difficult to be fully loving when you cannot remember and accept, without denial or self-punishment, that whatever you are now, you began life as a vulnerable and totally open child. You were completely dependent on your parents to survive physically and develop emotionally. Whatever ways in which you now struggle with anger, depression, guilt or resentment, it is essential to remember that you began life as a child. You could not be expected to see things from an adult point of view, make adult decisions or take the blame or responsibility for your family's problems.

This is what may be missing from your memories and from your life: the *feeling* awareness that you were once an innocent child. That is why so much of recovery from co-dependency centers on the rediscovery of your Inner Child.

The Inner Child

I have found the concept of the Inner Child to be very useful in healing from childhood trauma. For me the Inner Child is your intuitive, spontaneous, magical self who had to retreat into hiding to avoid the pain of your family environment. This child remains within you, waiting to grieve for all that he or she went through. Your Inner Child longs to be welcomed into the world again, to be loved and regarded.

Gradually opening yourself to your Inner Child can help you be gentle with yourself as you heal from your past. If you can keep your innocence in mind, you can begin to see that many of the disabling patterns you developed were the best survival strategies your intelligent, perceptive, sensitive child could devise to cope with confusing and impossible situations.

You can let go of blaming yourself and judging the attitudes and behaviors that served you as a child in a dysfunctional family, but no longer help you as an adult. If you find you are getting down on yourself for the way you have handled life in the past, remember you did the best you could with what you had to work with. In fact, many of your "liabilities" — the co-dependent behaviors that became the survival mechanisms of your childhood — can turn into your "assets." You must have been smart as a child to find the means to survive in a dysfunctional home. If you had not been a strong, resourceful, creative human being, you wouldn't be here to read this book now.

To understand better how your childhood has affected you, we will look at the ways in which you experience love as a child. We will see that when love becomes distorted in a dysfunctional home, you can behave in self-destructive ways and abandon your Inner Child.

How Children Learn About Love

As an infant you pass through what is called the *narcissistic stage*. This is an important step in your growth to becoming a healthy person. In order to develop healthy self-esteem, you need to be satisfied at the narcissistic stage by the full presence of a person who takes your needs seriously.

According to Alice Miller in her book, *The Drama of the Gifted Child*, when you are a child, you need: "respect, echoing, understanding, sympathy and mirroring" in order to feel a sense of "existential security." It is only by being nurtured in these ways that you successfully grow through the narcissistic stage to become a secure human being who is capable of appropriately caring for other people.

When your parents give you the attention and regard you need as an infant, you are able to explore and express your true self. You have the safety and encouragement to simply *be*. In particular, you are able to experience freely the wide range of your feelings. As an infant, you need to go through a stage of having all your emotions validated so that you can learn how to feel.

If your parents nurture you through the narcissistic stage, you will be able to maintain a sense of yourself as you grow older. Because you will have a solid sense of who you are, you will have less trouble separating or differentiating your personality from those of your parents. You will be comfortable sharing your feelings, thoughts, needs and wishes — all of which allow you to be alive and present with others in your life. When you can have your full self in this way, you will be able to give your love to others freely.

As we saw in the first chapter, if your parents did not receive the nurturing they needed and have not sought help to heal from their pasts, they will be unable to give you the unconditional regard that you need. Your parents may react to you as they would to an adult (usually their own parents.) Instead of supporting you to explore who you are, they may apply adult categories to your behavior, such as selfishness. Your parents may expect from you a regard for others that young children do not have, but must learn over time from their parents.

Along with imposing inappropriate restrictions on you, your parents can look to you for the love they did not receive as children. By using you to fulfill their emotional needs, your parents become cradle robbers. They snatch you from childhood before you receive the love and nurturing you need.

If you were deprived in this fashion, you become confused about how to love in a healthy way. You equate love with trying to take care of another person's unresolved issues. You take on the burden of your parents' problems and become enmeshed with your parents' identities (which are enmeshed with *their* parents' identities).

When you are taught to equate love with enmeshment, feeling empathy can become a threatening experience. There is too great a chance that if you allow yourself to feel for someone else, to listen with your true self, you will be overwhelmed by another person's problems. When you are abused and/or emotionally abandoned as a child, you are trapped. If you love, you end up overwhelmed. If you don't love, you are terrified of being abandoned. Unconscious fears of abandonment can haunt you throughout your life, blocking you from feeling and expressing the love in your heart.

Take Care Of Me — Or Else

Although your parents may not have been aware of their behavior, they may have turned to direct or indirect manipulation to get you to take care of them. Middelton-Moz and Dwinell cite the following messages that can intimidate you into becoming an emotional and physical caretaker of your parents:

- "I'm glad you're here. Take care of me." (Jael Greenleaf)
- "Your behavior can make me sick, crazy or kill me. I will die if you don't take care of me, leaving you with no one."
- "I will desert you or commit suicide if you don't take care of me." (paraphrase)

After The Tears

A few years ago I saw the effects of these messages on several of my clients in group therapy. I had some physical problems requiring exploratory surgery, and my clients were upset. As is normal and healthy, they were both concerned for me and worried about losing my support. A few of them began to act out the patterns of their childhoods. Unconsciously, they behaved as children who felt that their mother's sickness must be their fault. They felt that the way to help me was to suppress themselves, make sacrifices by denying their own emotional needs and controlling their expectations of me as a therapist. They felt as if their needing me had somehow made me sick.

I was able to recognize what was happening and to establish appropriate ways for them to care for me. I told them that I was prepared for the surgery and that what I needed was for them to be supportive in an adult way — pray for me, and call and let me know they are thinking of me. This, I told them, made me feel strengthened and cared for. There was no need for them to punish or suppress themselves.

This experience gave many of the group clients more self-esteem. They saw that they could help someone and be effective. Too often they were accustomed to trying to help their parents and feeling they failed to do so. Often they were asked, directly or indirectly, to help in ways beyond their understanding or capabilities. For example, many of them had learned to . . .

- Raise younger siblings because their parents were preoccupied with their own problems.
- Protect parents by making excuses for them and hiding their disease from siblings.
- Take the blame for fights and family tensions to help take the pressure off their parents.
- Let parents control them or overprotect them to relieve their parents' anxiety.
- Be a parent's confidant or take physical or sexual abuse in order to give the parent something he or she seemed to need desperately.

I listened to the following exchange between Amanda and her teenaged daughter, Cecilia, which brought to light the confusion that results from caretaking. Both women are now in treatment and were discussing how Amanda had been overprotective of Cecilia as a child, and how Cecilia had learned to become a caretaker. Amanda recalled how she had felt responsible for what were only the moods of her child. If Cecilia was fussy or was not nursing well, Amanda was sure that she was somehow at fault. This caused Amanda considerable anxiety. Amanda did not realize that her anxiety was heightened because the age of your child can reactivate the feelings you suppressed when you were the same age.

As a teenager Cecilia told her side of it. She said that from the earliest she could remember, she had been aware of her mother's worries. She had been fearful and later angry because she didn't know what to do about her mother's anxiety. On top of that Cecilia felt guilty for being angry with her mother.

Amanda modeled co-dependent behavior by taking responsibility for her baby's normal babyness, that included being fussy at times. Cecilia developed co-dependent thinking by taking responsibility for her mother's anxiety. In turn Amanda's anxiety increased further when Cecilia became upset. Both mother and daughter were caught in the vicious cycle of the disease.

The relationship between Louis and his father is another example of this confusion. Louis had a sense that he needed to cheer up his father who was often depressed. Sometimes it would work. One of his funny anecdotes about school would start his father laughing. However, Louis' influence on his father backfired. If his father remained depressed, Louis felt that it was his fault. This led Louis to believe that he was a bad person. It is a frightening burden as a child to think your parents are so fragile that you can control their moods.

Whether you're conscious of it or not, inappropriately taking care of your parents can lead to *black and white thinking, scapegoating* and *parentification.* All of these patterns can keep you from loving in healthy ways.

Emotional Chaos: Black And White Thinking

When you are intimidated into taking care of your parents as a child, you can develop what I call black and white thinking. As a young child, you are desperate to know whether or not your parents truly love you. You need their love as badly as oxygen or food. But in a dysfunctional family you do not get the unconditional love you need. Instead of being affirmed for who you are, your worth can seem to depend on whether you behave in the ways in which your parents need. This may lead you to doubt whether or not you are worthy of being loved. Remember, for a child this is a matter of survival. You are physically dependent on your parents and your identity is not clearly separated from theirs.

When you try to determine whether or not your parents love you, you can begin to categorize every action, every feeling and every thought of yours and you use them to determine whether you are "good" or "bad." There is no in-between, no shadings. It's absolute because to a child either you are loved and wanted or you're not. When you get older, you have the opportunity to learn how complicated life can be and how ambivalent people can be. You learn that it is possible to like some things a person does and dislike others. You start to realize, too, that you can still love someone even if you do not like his or her behavior.

Janet's story illustrates the effects of black and white thinking. She told me about her childhood experience with an alcoholic mother and how she coped with her fear and pain by attempting to be in control at all times.

"I always had the feeling," Janet explained, "that there was underlying tension and hostility between my parents (and that it often related to me), even when everything appeared to be peaceful. On one level I was always waiting for the next explosion to take place. However, I would hope that I was imagining the hostility and that everything was really all right. My parents reinforced my denial by saying that nothing was wrong when I would ask about something that had happened. I see now that there was never any conflict resolution since we didn't talk openly, and we never tried on a day-to-day basis to clear up the hurt feelings. As each year passed I became less and less able to trust my feelings."

As a result, Janet learned to deny and repress her feelings, to be in control as a defense against chaotic family behaviors. One way in which she was able to control her feelings was by categorizing them.

Another client, Tom, also developed this pattern of thinking because of the way in which his mother treated him. Her attitude was extreme.

Tom told me, "Either my mother loved me or she hated me. Either I was good or I was worthless. Depending on how she treated me at any given time, I was either wonderful or stupid. Everything in life was going to go fine without a hitch or everything was going to go wrong. People were either decent and lovable, or evil and despicable. I could trust a friend 100 percent — or not at all."

This way of thinking prevented Tom and Janet from being overwhelmed by their perceptions and emotions. They used this defense to keep their emotional life in order and to protect themselves.

Categorizing their feelings had a detrimental effect on Tom and Janet as they grew up. Their perceptions of people were often distorted. They were unable to understand people's complexity or to be compassionate with their flaws. If a boy at school was nice to him, Tom immediately tried to make him a "best friend" who could do no wrong. If another boy did something he didn't approve of, Tom immediately wrote him off as a jerk without a single good quality. At home his mother might still rage, erratically loving or hating Tom, but in the emotional world Tom could control, good was good and bad was bad, and there was no room for even a hint of chaos.

Perhaps you also think in extremes. If so, you may not clearly remember when you started thinking like this.

Phillip had a clear memory of trying to puzzle out his mother's verbal abuse when he was six years old. He remembered being lost in confusing thoughts and deciding that he must be worthless. Tracy remembered clearly the day in fifth grade when she decided never to express her feelings to her mother again. Ted knew that by age nine he was writing nasty little satires of friends and school, already deciding some things were stupid. He took great joy in the sense of control and safety it gave him to pass absolute judgments on the confusing complicated world around him.

Black and white thinking is harmful to your spirit and your life in many ways. At any age you hurt yourself when you feel compelled to decide absolutely whether someone or something is good or bad. You may be dealing with a friend, a parent, a lover or a spouse. You may be trying to get involved in a group, a company, an institution or a political organization. If you're favorably impressed at first, you will decide it's good — absolutely good, perfect — and you will plunge in with total commitment and trust until the first imperfection shows up. The first time someone or something you have idolized shows its clay feet, the first time your hero gets a cold or your lover does something selfish, they become irredeemably bad. So you resent them or run away and suffer anxiety and uncertainty, unable to figure out what you really feel about them.

Until you are strong enough to accept that every person has both assets and liabilities, you will have a hard time relating to people on an intimate level. Understanding that no one is all good or all bad is part of learning how to care for others appropriately without hurting yourself.

You can begin to free yourself from black and white thinking and its hurtful consequences by recognizing its origins in your past. As a child you were simply trying to defend yourself against the inconsistent behavior and unresolved pain of a dysfunctional parent.

Scapegoats Take The Heat

Scapegoating is a common way in which parents look to their children to take care of the parents' problems. Scapegoating involves blaming, accusing and generally focusing on the negative behavior of one person. Families will also focus on suspected negative behavior. One person is always under suspicion: he or she is the troublemaker of the family who cannot be trusted.

Scapegoating can be more severe in some families than in others, and the way in which a family member is cast in the scapegoat role may be largely unconscious. Family members may not be aware they are avoiding their own problems by blaming them on a scapegoat. The family sees the scapegoat's distracting, interrupting, unacceptable behavior as the problem. The parents tell the child, "You're uncooperative!" instead of looking at what demands they are placing on the child or what is going on between the parents to which the child could be reacting.

Pam became the scapegoat in her dysfunctional family. Her mother was an alcoholic, and her father would not address his wife's disease. Instead, both her father and mother blamed Pam for their discomforts and the tension in their marriage. There was no time for them to look at themselves. They had their hands full dealing with Pam. From kindergarten on she was a problem child, not getting along with others, not doing well in class and giving her teachers a hard time.

Pam's parents were frequently sarcastic, threatening and critical of her. They gave scant attention to anything positive she did. Instead of talking openly with her and giving consequences for specific unacceptable behavior, they generalized from her negative behavior that she was simply "bad."

"What's she done now?" was her mother's sarcastic comment whenever Pam misbehaved.

Even though your misbehavior can have negative repercussions for yourself and your family, by taking on the role of scapegoat you are being an extremely loyal family member. You are living in accordance with "invisible loyalties." By acting out the unresolved tensions in your home, you hold the family together and protect it from its own stress.

In this role you are a lightning rod for your family. Rick remembers having a dim sense when he was eight years old that the more his parents told him he was bad and a failure, the more he miserably clung to them out of love and loyalty.

"I distinctly recall," he said, "feeling almost proud of myself for letting my mother yell at me. It seemed to make her feel better, and I wanted her to be happy. I'd tell myself it was good that she got it out of her system."

Constantly taking the blame for family tensions can make you feel as though you are a bad person. This can become your identity. You may develop a deeply ingrained sense of shame. No matter what, when anything goes wrong, or looks as though it could go wrong, you can feel ashamed because it was somehow your fault.

In one family I know, Larry, a scapegoated young child, was ready to take the blame for whatever bad thing he had done as soon as he saw his father come home with a frown on his face. His father may have been frowning because the rush hour traffic happened to be particularly hectic that day. But Larry felt that, somehow, anything that had upset his father must have been his fault. As he grew older, Larry developed an ingrained pattern of blaming himself whenever anyone frowned or seemed upset.

Once you fall into the role of a scapegoat or making someone else into a scapegoat, it becomes a habit with its own distorted rewards. For a young child, being a scapegoat is often the only way to get attention. Even negative attention is better than no attention at all.

I pointed out to Wendy, a young mother struggling with her desperate need for control, that she often ignored her four-year-old girl except to shout, "Don't do that. Be quiet." As a result, the affection-starved child became adept at doing things that irritated her mother — from whining to playing with things she was not supposed to touch. When no verbal warning could stop her, punishment was necessary. This confirmed Wendy's belief that a parent has to be firmly in control. For the little girl the punishment was the price she had to pay for enjoying a few minutes of her mother's attention.

A scapegoated child also gains a certain amount of power and adult status. As a scapegoat you sense that you, a child, are very important to these adults. Although you are labeled as irresponsible, many things seem to depend upon you. Beneath your role, you can carry a big responsibility for a child.

The importance of a scapegoat in a dysfunctional family can be seen by the fact that often, as soon as one child grows into a teenager and leaves, the next oldest child suddenly falls from parental favor and becomes the new scapegoat. But the scapegoat is not necessarily always a child.

Sometimes the target of scapegoating is a spouse, which usually results in dysfunction in that spouse. Spouses may take turns being the scapegoat. Often someone who was scapegoated as a child will continue to play the scapegoat role in a marriage. Cultural biases determine who fills the role. In marital conflicts many cultures, including our own, tend to blame the woman. If a man is abusing her, it is assumed that she must have provoked it. If the man leaves her, it must have been her fault.

When you assume responsibility for the conflicts of your family, your physical health can be affected. According to Sharon Wegscheider-Cruse in her tape, *Co-dependency: The Trap and the Triumph*, "The body will cry out for what your mind distorts and your feelings repress."

In young children problems such as hyperactivity, asthma, allergies and systemic cancers, such as Hodgkin's

Disease and leukemia, may be be related to co-dependent patterns of family life. The child's sickness can function to take care of the family by absorbing its pain and tension. When a child is sick, the family's unresolved emotional tensions can continue to be ignored because there is a sick child to look after.

Scapegoats And Medication

When a scapegoated child begins to show "problem behavior," people often seek a pharmaceutical solution to control it.

In *After The Tears*, Middelton-Moz and Dwinell sum up the three positions that professionals often take regarding problem behavior and depression:

1. The problem is neurophysiological — a genetically determined imbalance that can only be corrected pharmaceutically.
2. The problem is one of learned behavior, requiring behavior modification techniques.
3. The problem is psychological, requiring individual or family therapy.

Professionals who adhere to the medical model — that the problem is one of neurophysiology — may not recognize that a person has been cast as a scapegoat and that the person's problem behavior is protecting the family from its unresolved tensions. As a result a physician may treat the individual with tranquilizers, antidepressants and antipsychotics but leave the dysfunctional family system intact.

Many problem behaviors respond to family therapy with a therapist who is highly knowledgeable in addictive family systems. In many cases drugs mask the family problem and do not solve the problem behavior. Drugs should never be allowed to take away your true feelings. It is important to feel your pain about your family situation. There is a message in the pain.

There are instances when a drug is appropriate for a child. For example, there are certain biologically based disorders such as obsessive compulsive disorder, attention deficit disorder, unipolar depression, manic depression (bipolar disorder) and dysthynia (a continuing, but not incapacitating, depression) that when diagnosed by specially trained clinicians, can be helped by appropriate medication. However, if handled competently, the medication is usually administered after a thorough investigation into all areas of the child's life. It is also used in conjunction with behavior modification, new parenting skills plus individual and family therapy.

There are many ways to look at what is meant by problem behavior. If you cannot function in society, then perhaps some form of medication may be helpful. But if the problem is your feelings are upsetting someone else, then you are being medicated to solve *their* problem. If this is the case, another form of help would be better. For instance, 12-Step programs are very effective in helping family members to heal from many types of dysfunctional behavior.

Little Parents

Parentification is another exploitation of children that distorts their understanding of love. When you are "parentified," other members of the family, as well as people outside the family, see you as the ideal child. You play the role of the family hero. You are given undue responsibility for healing and nurturing your parents or resolving their problems. You are treated as a special child, being asked frequently to be a parent to your parents, as well as your siblings. You are asked to take care of your parents' feelings and needs.

Except in sexual matters, such an occasional role reversal between you and your parents is a natural part of growing up and is necessary for you to learn as a child how to be empathetic and responsible. However, when it becomes a regular way of relating, the parent exploits the child. Regardless of how appealing this position appears to be for the child, it retards emotional growth and is very confusing to the child.

Learning to see your parents as human beings is an important part of growing up. It is healthy to develop this perspective as you establish your individual adult identity. When this happens too early, however, it can be too great a burden. In a life tragedy — the death of a parent, for example — an adult provider or caretaker role may be thrust on a child. Going to work or raising, clothing and feeding siblings may come earlier than expected. In dire circumstances many children have to grow up quickly. If you must give up your childhood because your parents are alcoholic, undependable or broken down in some way, you are learning to put others' needs ahead of your own in an inappropriate and unhealthy way.

When Sid was eight years old, he was terrified one night when his mother overdosed on the prescription drugs to which she was addicted. His father's denial about his wife's problem was very strong. Despite the obvious signs that her life was in peril, Sid's father refused to take action. Sid had to argue with, entreat and threaten his father to call the hospital. Sid was placed in a position of responsibility that was clearly inappropriate for a child.

As with any part of the disease of co-dependency, parentification may be passed on from one generation to the next. In some families passing on the family behavior is openly encouraged. A parent may tell the child, "I obeyed my parents. You obey me. And your children will obey you." In other families this is more unconscious. A parent can put demands on a child without being aware they are inappropriate. With treatment this cycle can be broken, and children can mature at a healthy natural pace.

Healthy And Unhealthy Helping Out

It is important to see that there are ways children can be expected to appropriately help their parents. There are times when parents have a legitimate need for help. It is also healthy for parents to ease their children into taking responsibility for household chores, yard work and generally making a contribution to the home and family. It is a hard job to raise a child. But it is also a hard job for the child to learn many of the difficult tasks demanded by the adult world and to integrate them emotionally without damaging self-esteem.

To help with this process, parents can learn to ask children to help out in age-appropriate ways. It is damaging to ask children to do things that are beyond them intellectually, emotionally or physically. Children have a natural love of their parents and if encouraged, enjoy helping and feeling as though they are an important part of the family's activities.

I know of a family that runs a small breakfast stop in the outer suburbs. Every morning truckers and others stop on their way to work for breakfast. An older couple is the core of the operation with their grown-up children helping out from time to time — partly to help their parents, partly to make some extra money. A son away at college, for example, usually helps out in the summer.

One of the daughters who works there is married and has a baby girl, Tricia. Before she could walk, Tricia slept in a crib by the cash register, looking out with big eyes at all the customers who smiled at her and thought she was as cute as a button. As soon as she became a toddler, her mother let her walk about the diner, always under supervision. Surrounded by walls of snacks, toys and candy bars, Tricia had to learn "not to touch" pretty quickly. The family loved her and gave her lots of affection.

By age two Tricia was demanding to be part of the action and to help out. When her grandfather and delivery men were stocking the coolers with soft drinks and milk cartons, Tricia would come to help out. They would encourage her to help place cartons on the cooler racks. She would gallantly carry a milk carton — getting a little unseen help from behind and lots of verbal encouragement — and feel a part of things. By helping in these ways, Tricia's abilities were validated and she learned how to be responsible.

In healthy families like Tricia's, parents are alert for appropriate ways a child can contribute and learn to express caring. If the mother gets sick, for example, and is in bed with the flu, she might ask her young child to take care of her in an age-appropriate way by bringing her some soup or getting milk from the store. What makes this a healthy caring action is that the child is being asked to do something appropriate to a child — a task within his or her comprehension. At the same time the mother is reassuring the child that she is still the parent and will be all right. The child learns that his or her actions and contributions can be effective in helping someone, but does not have to feel that the parents are completely dependent on the child.

It would be inappropriate if the mother is "sick" all the time because of her alcoholism or depression, for example, and needs the child to prepare all her meals. In this case, the child is not getting reassurance that the parent is in control and nurturing. Instead the child feels that the mother cannot take care of herself and the child must be the parent. Unhealthy parents will reinforce this feeling in their child. If the child is not blamed, he or she is led to believe that the parent has problems with the world or other people (relatives, for example) that make the parent sick. Children who must be this kind of caretaker sacrifice their own needs for being nurtured and learn that other people's emotional needs must come first.

In sum, parents need to think clearly, without co-dependent distortions, about what kind of help and support they need and should be able to expect. They need to look at where this support should come from, how much from spouse and children, and how to ask for support. Our society is slowly becoming aware that it places too much pressure on the nuclear family. Support structures (cultural opportunities, day care, counseling, etc.), which were less available in the past, are absolutely necessary to take impossible burdens off parents. These burdens are often the triggers for outbreaks of co-dependent behavior.

Parents certainly may feel justified in asking children to help out with chores around the house. As we have seen, this teaches responsibility and a spirit of cooperation. But parents may want to take it as a warning sign of co-dependent thinking when they ask children to "not be a problem" and behave "correctly," without regard for the individual child. The parents' motivation may not be to help the child, but to maintain their self-image as good parents and defend themselves against any accusations that they are not fulfilling their role as parents. This is especially true if the parent is not meeting basic parental obligations to the child because of alcoholism, drug addiction, workaholism, gambling, overeating or other addictions.

Self-Parenting

To begin to recover from your dysfunctional childhood, it is helpful to connect with your Inner Child. Because this child was so deeply wounded in the past, you may have lost conscious access to him or her. Through therapy and by becoming your own parent, you can begin to open the door to your Inner Child.

Honoring the wounded child within you does not mean that you live in a child-like state. You still need to function as an adult and take responsibility for yourself on a daily basis. In time you can learn to integrate your Inner Child into your adult life and reclaim your creative, curious and playful nature.

To make it safe for your Inner Child to begin to come out, you need to be in an environment that is free of toxic people (people whose dysfunction and behavior towards you undermine your efforts at self-love). If you are around people who abuse you, you need to get away from them or stand up for yourself in an appropriate way. Your Inner Child needs the protection of a self-responsible adult: you!

Self-parenting means taking care of your Inner Child the way you would take care of a real child. It is not healthy to apply repressive, dysfunctional rules ("Be quiet! Sit down!"), but rather use love and sensitivity ("I hear you. I hear your feelings. It's not okay for someone to talk abusively to you"). What children need most is access to their feelings and for the full range of their feelings to be heard.

In the same way your Inner Child needs to be able to express all of his or her feelings — not only love and caring, but anger and terror. It may be challenging for you to let your Inner Child feel rage (pain and fear) that the world was not the way he or she wanted it to be. If you can honor your Inner Child's feelings, talk about the dis-ease of co-dependency and offer reassurance that you are there to protect him or her today, you can make it safe for your Inner Child to emerge from hiding.

Frozen Feelings

You can begin to free yourself from what Wayne Krits-berg calls *chronic shock*.

When you grow up in any kind of dysfunctional home, you live through traumatic events without resolving the effects of those experiences. As a result you are left with frozen feelings. If you do not work through them, the feelings remain stuck in your body for the rest of your life. You live in a state of chronic shock.

Human beings naturally go into shock when they are seriously threatened. The purpose of this is to keep you from being overwhelmed or going insane. According to Kritsberg, this process takes place in three stages:

1. When you first go into shock, your body becomes numb. The color leaves your face and your eyes become vacant and distant. Adrenaline pours through your system.
2. Next is the recoil phase when your feelings, such as terror, loss or grief, emerge. This phase can last anywhere from a matter of hours to several months.

3. Finally you process your emotions by discharging them and talking about them with supportive people. You can then integrate the experience into your life. You see that, although painful things will happen to you, you can learn from them and grow as a person.

The Adult Children of Alcoholics Syndrome

When you live through a trauma in a dysfunctional home, your body shuts down as you enter the first stage of shock. But because of the rigid rules by which you learn to live, you are unable to move through the initial shock to the following stages and to express your feelings about what happened. The family environment is not safe enough to support you, and the no-talk rule leaves you isolated and left to try to interpret the event as best you can. You remain in the initial shock phase.

People in chronic shock talk about scenes from their past as though they were scenes from a movie they had watched. They are completely detached from their emotions. If you think back to an event in your past, you may be able to get a sense of how you cut off from your feelings. Have you ever recounted a terrifying incident from your past with a steady voice and no sign of emotion?

Kelly told me of a time, at age six, when her drunken mother drove into the driveway and smashed her car into the garage. Kelly ran to the garage and saw her mother unconscious, slumped over the steering wheel. Kelly's first thought was that her mother was dead. The little girl went into shock. The next day her mother seemed fine and the garage was fixed. No one talked about what had happened. Kelly had no way to work through her feelings of terror. Other people have told me of verbal, physical or sexual abuse, or witnessing abuse between parents and siblings, that created a feeling of helplessness that was repressed.

When you live in a state of chronic shock, where does the trapped emotional energy go? It stays stuck in your system, unrecognized for what it is. Your range of feelings narrows and you do not have access to the nuances of emotional experiences. A part of you shuts down and stays shut down. That part becomes an adversary, a phantom lurking within you that you must guard against at all times. On an unconscious level when you start to have strong feelings, your body says: "Uh-oh, here come a lot of emotions; it's time to go numb!"

This is true for joyful emotions as well as painful ones. Clients have told me how they went through the motions of their wedding or the christening of a child without feeling anything. It is also common for people in chronic shock to equate joy with the absence of pain. They assume that if their lives are temporarily free from crises, they must be happy.

This continuing state of shock can set in at an early age. I've seen the light go out of children between the ages of six and 13. Before this, they're spunky and uncorrupted. Children are not afraid to speak out and to call a spade a spade: "Daddy, I'm angry because you drink too much!" But something happens. Their spirit seems to die. Somehow the family system finally overwhelms them. By their early teenage years they are often drinking to medicate the pain. Their thoughts are confused and their feelings blocked. They may live in a state of denial, or they may say with cynicism or bitterness that love and spirituality are useless, and feelings are for the weak.

But the Inner Child never really dies. Your Inner Child hides deep inside, wounded, guarding his or her love and ability to empathize, afraid of the light until you are ready to offer a helping hand.

Wounded Child, Wise Child

The child within you will know if you continue to abandon him or her. That child will continue to act out until you listen to the child's feelings and needs. It is a paradox, but you will feel more powerful and alive when you acknowledge the vulnerable child within you.

If you allow your Inner Child to feel the full range of feelings, and you try to satisfy his or her needs in a reasonable way as a healthy parent would do, you will find that your Inner Child is not only hurt and wounded from the past, but is also a source of wisdom.

As a child I always knew there was something better than what I had in life, that it was possible to have healthy, intimate relationships. This was not an intellectual belief, but a knowing deep inside. In recovery I have experienced the parenting I always knew was possible, and I have found intimacy in relationships. My Inner Child now tells me, "Yes, this is what I've always wanted. Thank you."

To get in touch with this insight and wisdom, I had to learn to open up to all of my feelings and to accept the ambiguity of conflicting emotions. I had to be a parent who could really be there for my Inner Child. Then I learned that my wounded child was also a wise child from whom I had much to learn.

Some Things To Do: Your Inner Child

Find a safe quiet place where no one will disturb you. If you can, I recommend you record the following guided imagery on a tape which you can listen to whenever you want:

Go inside and visualize a place where you feel safe. It may be the woods, a meadow, the mountains, by the ocean, anywhere you choose.

Take a few deep breaths.

Feel the energy in the universe, feel it pulsating around you . . . and in you . . . continue to breathe.

See if you can contact your little child inside you. Whatever age you see is fine.

Visualize that child in the safe space you have created.

Take a few more deep breaths.

If you are unable to visualize your Inner Child, do not make yourself wrong for that. It's okay if you cannot see that child yet. That will come in time. Just let yourself have a sense of that child's spirit and be with him or her for a few minutes. Continue to breathe.

If you would like, take your child's hand and go for a little walk.

If you want to talk to the child, please do. Tell the child the truth, whatever it is that you say.

Take a couple of deep breaths.

Perhaps you would be willing to find a comfortable spot and sit down and ask your child if you can hold him or her.

Continue to breathe.

While you are holding this child, you may wish to say something to him or her, something perhaps this child has wanted to hear for a long time.

If you choose, say to the child,

- "I am glad you are alive."

- "I am glad you were born."

- "I am glad you are a girl" or "I am glad you are a boy."

- "Just being is enough."

- "There's plenty of time."

Just sit with your child for a few moments and feel the warmth and closeness.

I invite you to say to your child that you will take him or her with you as you leave this safe place, that you will keep your child's presence with you.

You may want to build into your daily life rituals with the child. Put your little child next to you in your car when you are driving (using the seat belt, of course). Take him or her to the park with you. Walk through the grass in bare feet and smell the flowers. Feed the ducks. Let yourself truly be with your innocent, alive, curious child.

Tuck your child in at night, and talk to him or her. Ask your child how the day went and how he or she is feeling. Perhaps read your Inner Child a story.

If you know you are going somewhere that is not safe for your little child, explain where you are going, why you are going and when you will be back. Leave your child in a safe place with a "baby-sitter" — this could be your cat, your teddy bear, your own spirit or even a friend who understands the importance of nurturing your little child.

I also encourage you to say one or two of the affirmations to yourself every day for a week. Go on to another affirmation the following week, and so on. Say them in the morning and at night. When you say them, look at yourself in the mirror. Really look into your eyes and see your soul. See your face. Study it lovingly, accept its uniqueness. Really see the person who is there and regard him or her.

This may feel awkward at first. That's okay. If you are willing, try it for a little while. See how it feels to you and see how your Inner Child responds. If you give it time, you may come to enjoy nurturing yourself and your little child.

3

Teen Twists

If you grow up in a dysfunctional home, you reach a crossroads when you become a teenager. As an adolescent you have more control and personal power in your life and more consciousness about your actions. You have more options, more freedom and less physical and financial dependence than you did when you were a young child. This is a time when you decide whether to go forward into a new life or pour more energy into rescuing your parents and trying to heal your family's pain.

As you enter adolescence, you can become emotionally crippled if you try to take care of your troubled parents. Your problems at home can interfere with natural maturing activities, such as spending time with friends and coping with school. The guilt, anger, resentment and enmeshed relationships within your dysfunctional home can interfere with these processes. Excessive unconscious loyalties can cloud each stage of growth.

As a teenager you can threaten the family system when you begin to question its values and beliefs. Your questioning may undermine the family's need to maintain its myths and protect its members from facing the pain of their own lost childhoods.

If your parents are severely co-dependent, you can expect resistance and negative messages about your physical maturation, your decisions about love, your choice of friends and lifestyle, and the social and ethical values of your peers. The development of your unique personality can threaten family members who feel safe in the enmeshment of a dysfunctional home.

Your transition from child to adult requires negotiation, trial flights from the nest, taking the initiative to be independent, asking for help and building relationships with people outside of your family. A dysfunctional family system resists each of these steps.

As a teenager you also need to be able to try on new identities. This is the only way to learn who you are. But trying new things means having the freedom and support to make mistakes. This will probably not be possible in a troubled family that lives by rigid rules and expectations that are cast in concrete over generations. An inherited identity can wait for you, like a straightjacket. Your own thinking is likely to be defensive, frightened and black and white about finding the "right" way to be.

In a dysfunctional home your parents may become dictatorial and say no to any request because they are inflexible and unable to weigh each decision on its own merits.

At the other extreme they may be afraid to ever say no. Because dysfunctional parents basically want your approval, they may not set appropriate limits on your behavior. Their fear of your anger can keep them from giving you the guidance and modeling you need through your adolescence.

As you grow into an adult in a dysfunctional family system, you will probably not be able to draw on your feelings and spiritual knowledge for guidance. Your state of chronic shock and denial about your life can keep you from your true self. Instead of seeking help, you may turn to rebellion, depression, even suicide — all of which our addictive society is quick to accept as normal for an adolescent.

The legacy of a co-dependent childhood can be like a heavy weight inside you as a teenager and young adult. You can struggle with the inexplicable terrifying feeling that you do not know how to be close with another person, are somehow not being true to yourself and are living a false life. Cut off from your Inner Child, you may look for an answer for your haunting disease. You may search in many places and not find an answer until you seek treatment and begin to retrieve your true self.

Marti's Summer Of Love

Marti, an exceptionally kind and thoughtful person, told me of some of the devastating experiences she went through as a teenager trying to cope with her mother's alcoholism. Her story reveals the intensity of the struggle for young people when they take on the burden of their parents.

"Throughout my childhood," Marti told me, "I believed that if I were better behaved in some undefined way, my mother would not be sick. This belief was reinforced by my mother who was extremely critical and controlling. She often blamed me for her problems and told me I was a bad person. When I became a teenager, I was obsessed with what I now call 'magic healing.' I was haunted by the idea that by absorbing my mother's pain and controlling her feelings, I could make her well.

"As an adolescent I applied my maturing intellect to my mother's problems by avidly reading about mysticism and the power of mind control. Looking back, I see that I was confused about the limits of such mental activities in changing the world, but I was obsessed with the idea that my thoughts could help others, especially my mother.

"I was in a state of great pain over this, but when I thought about giving up on trying to heal my mother, an inner voice of guilt would nag at me, 'It is your mission to make your mother better.'

"I felt selfish for wanting to put energy into anything of my own as long as I knew my mother needed me. I felt a twinge of guilt that was barely conscious for every class I attended, every date I went on and every simple pleasure I allowed myself. I wouldn't even permit myself to enjoy the beauty of a sunny day or a beautiful flower as I walked to class."

Marti had a wonderful gift of empathy but because of faulty thinking, unclear boundaries and a lack of self-esteem, her natural empathy evolved into self-destructive caretaking. Marti was unable to separate herself from her mother in a healthy way. She believed she could feel her mother's pain. Marti did not realize that she was feeling her own pain, but mistook it for her mother's. Marti's feelings left her obsessed with trying to heal her mother.

"One summer when I was 19, I decided that once and for all, I would get my mother well. I completely repressed my feelings and tried to please her in every way possible. Maybe I just hadn't tried hard enough before, I reasoned. This time I gave everything I had. I went along with everything she wanted and tried to see her side in every-thing. I desperately tried to understand her irrational attitudes and behaviors.

"Whenever my desires for my own life emerged, I would push them down. I lived in a strangely depressed, yet at times exhilarated state. I believed in a popular way of thinking which claimed that I was all-powerful, that I was indeed God. I believed I was part of a healing beam of energy from the universe which I could direct at my mother. I thought if I performed just the right kind of behaviors and mental disciplines not to upset her equil-ibrium, she would get well. I believed I could 'think' her back to health. In my mind, having selfish or resentful thoughts, showing strong emotions, laughing at the wrong time, arguing with my father and becoming sex-ual in any way with my boyfriend could all cause my mother more pain."

Instead of improving her mother's health, Marti only damaged herself. Her mother was no better by the end of the summer and Marti returned to college with anxiety attacks.

"At college I had eruptions of feelings periodically that seemed to crash over me like a tidal wave. A letter or phone call from my mother usually triggered these episodes. I would feel the old sense of worthlessness and despair rise up again. These feelings seemed to come in an exaggerated, condensed form. They stood in stark contrast to the happy self that I could be when I had no contact with my mother. When the episodes of despair occurred, I felt that everything was closing in on me. I felt a dark badness inside of me because I had not saved my mother.

"I finally decided to get help. I went to talk with a priest several times and with a psychiatrist. They both said I was fine, that I understood my mother's situation and that I simply had to go on with my life from there. This was not possible for me to do at the time — it was not as simple as that. My mother was still alive and I still held out hope that, somehow, I could help her to get well."

Marti was haunted by a terrible sense of guilt and obligation. She was carrying a lot of her mother's shame and suffering. She felt responsible for her mother's illness and the healthy drives to grow up and create her own life were sapped by the sense of wrongdoing and unfinished business at home. She kept thinking that she had abandoned her mother, that she had not done enough, tried enough and given her all to make her mother well.

Marti's attempts to reach out for help did not relieve her of this burden. Unfortunately the priest and the psychiatrist she went to had little knowledge of addictions and co-dependency. They could only see that Marti understood her situation on an intellectual level. They were unable to address her deeper issues. They reassured her that she "had her act together" because she could explain her mother's condition. This reassurance only led Marti to think that she might be crazy. Marti reasoned that since she understood the situation, she should not be having dark feelings and obsessive thoughts.

Unfortunately despite the greater availability of help and support today, Marti's experience is still a common one. Marti did not know she was suffering from co-dependency. What Marti needed was encouragement to feel and express her feelings, help to cope with her dysfunctional family and in-depth treatment for her disease. As clergy and professionals continue to learn about addictions and co-dependency (and heal themselves in these areas), they will be better able to help people similar to Marti avoid years of needless suffering.

"You're Incapable Of Love"

As with Marti, when you are continually exposed to negative messages about yourself from your parents and family, you internalize and carry them as part of your identity. These negative messages are one way in which the shame and suffering of your parents is passed down to you.

Janice often told me, "I'm just not capable of being loving." This was her primary complaint when she entered therapy. She said that she felt she had not been loving enough to her parents. She had been labeled as "cold" and "aloof" by her family. She grew up feeling as though she were somehow different from other people, that she could not offer anything to others.

She had a lot of repressed anger she was not aware of, so she did not feel loving. After working through much of her anger and relating to people in group therapy for over two years, Janice began to see that she was indeed a loving person. She had plenty of love to give, but she had never been safe enough to let it out. The love had been even more repressed than the anger. Her group experience gave her the support she needed to let out the truly loving person hidden beneath her defenses.

Nick was also damaged by the messages he received growing up. If he disagreed with his mother or tried to negotiate with her, she would shout at him, "You're incapable of love!" Nick felt so ashamed by his mother's attacks that he sought to prove that he was indeed a caring and loving person. He went looking for other people to care for and to boost his low self-esteem. He felt drawn to people who were depressed, out of control and having a hard time coping. His first high school crowd was composed of such misfits. Nick tried to comfort them with a hug or a shoulder to cry on. He was, in a sense, putting out a small fire because he couldn't cope with the big one at home. This pattern of rescuing others continued to dominate his life and distort his thinking. He was unconsciously driven to try to take away people's pain in order to prove to his mother that he was a loving person.

Co-dependent One Liners

As a child it is easy to fall prey to irrational attacks as Nick did. If you grew up being criticized, you are probably susceptible to what I call *Co-dependent One Liners*. If you hear these from others or say them yourself, you may want to take notice. They invariably indicate that the person is speaking out of co-dependency. Here are some of the more common attacks:

- "If you really loved me, you'd _____."
- "You love _____ more than me."
- "You're so selfish."
- "You think you're perfect."
- "You always want everything your way."
- "You always have to be right."
- "I can't say anything right for you."
- "You never tell me anything."
- "All you want is my money."
- "I do all the work around here."

When you hear these kinds of attacks, you are probably listening to your own or to another's disease. If you can keep from engaging in irrational arguments and stand up for yourself in an appropriate way, you can learn to ward

off these attacks. In time you will be able to see through
these messages.

One way to respond to any of these statements is to
say, "I hear you are upset. Let's sit down and talk about it."
It is not healthy to continue to listen to abuse, but it is
appropriate to listen to the person's concerns if he or she
is willing to share in a responsible way.

Rigid Rules And Brittle Feelings

Along with the negative messages you receive in a
dysfunctional home, the rigid rules that helped your family to survive through the generations can turn against
you as you strive to become your own person. These
rules can restrict your spiritual growth and bury your
loving heart.

When Tim was in high school, he learned quickly that
one of his family's rules was, *Don't rock the boat.*

Tim told me, "My parents were concerned because I
was moving in a 'fast crowd.' As far as I could tell, that
meant we weren't afraid to go new places and try new
things. But it was clear I was making my parents very
nervous. They were disappointed in me for not behaving
as 'intellectually' as they knew I could. I wasn't interpreting
their frowns and grimaces and curtailing my time with
my friends, so they had to talk to me.

"My father took me aside and explained how my behavior was worrying my mother. He said I was making things
difficult for her.

"If I gave my mother an opening, she would tell me how
upset my father was, 'although he may not show it.' On
top of that, she'd plead with me to make things easier for
her. She was having a hard time, she said, dealing with my
father! I had a hard time understanding what they were
trying to tell me.

"Eventually I put together my own theory: Don't rock
the boat. Apparently they believed our family was so un-

stable, it couldn't handle the comradeship and excitement I felt in meeting some new friends.

"I didn't stop going out, but I felt guilty and resentful. That probably made me act out more. It certainly made me inconsiderate. I would refuse to call to let them know where I was or when I would be home. I didn't want them to control me by making me feel guilty.

"Because my parents were so unreasonable, I stopped letting them meet my friends, which only increased their worry and suspicion. I didn't want to bring friends home just to have my parents be critical and sarcastic. The few times I did bring a friend over, they embarrassed the hell out of me.

"In the end our communications broke down. I felt I didn't care for them at all. My apparent lack of love for them made me feel awful. I'd tell myself that it was a normal part of growing up but I had too many friends who got along fine with their parents to believe that. Although I was angry, I felt too guilty and afraid to talk to anyone about what was going on in our family. I gave up and figured that caring for anyone was futile.

"Deep inside this coldness felt terrible. It distorted my relationships with friends and lovers until I was well into my twenties when I began to be more independent of my parents. At that time, with the help of Adult Children of Alcoholics meetings, an excellent therapist and eventually co-dependency treatment, I was able to begin to sort out my past. I began to put all the confusion of my past into a clearer perspective."

Lisa also fell prey to dysfunctional rules. Her family lived by a common restriction in unhealthy families: *Don't trust anyone outside the family.* This rule helps to preserve the closed, enmeshed system by shutting out the outside world.

"My mother," Lisa said, "attempted to absorb the unspoken fears of our family. It took me years to learn all the painful facts of our family history and to realize that my mother was the one entrusted with this powder keg. It resembled a collage of fears built out of a child's nightmares. There was a great-grandfather who had committed suicide, a second cousin who had married someone from the 'wrong' religion and an uncle who had cheated on his wife and died young from alcoholism.

"The stories from my mother's immediate family may have been the most frightening. For example, my mother remembered one day when she was a little girl when her father beat her brother. This made such an impression on her that she was still afraid of her father's wrath when she was 40 years old, and he was already dead. She remained stuck as a little girl, still trembling before her abusive father.

"Learning our family's dark secrets affected me deeply when I went to school and met new people. I saw every person as a threat to my family. In my mind I could hear my family worrying, 'Is this the person who will see through us? The one who will expose the shame in our family and bring our house tumbling down?' I became so protective of my family that I was afraid to get too close to anyone. I thought it wasn't safe to trust anybody until I knew them as intimately as I knew the members of my family. Later I realized this was absurd because I didn't really know the members of my family!

"I was in my mid-teens when my mother became increasingly paranoid. She would verbally attack my activities and friends. I can still recall, decades later, the types of characters she created. She really thought there were people out there whose sole purpose was to do in our family. I knew my mother was paranoid and would feel physically sick with fear, pity and despair. The images she planted in my mind remained for years, as did her accusations that I was bad or working against her whenever I made friends with anyone new."

For both Tim and Lisa the rigid rules of their families led to a breakdown of communication and caring when they became teenagers and started to reach beyond their families. Their growth and new experiences triggered the anxieties of their families and led their parents to try to control them. Unable to share openly, they grew accustomed to indirect ways of communicating.

For instance, Tim was used to relating in triangles, where one parent would take him aside and confide in him about the other parent. For both Tim and Lisa, any effort to resolve the tension in the family always seemed to end in arguments and a breakdown of family bonding.

"I might as well be an orphan!" Lisa would yell at her mother.

"I wash my hands of you," Tim's father would yell at him.

But neither family was able to address the real issues beneath their conflicts: the enmeshment within the family due to behavior patterns passed down through the generations. This enmeshment blocked any efforts Lisa and Tim made to establish their own identities.

Of course there are dangers in the world and it is appropriate for parents to give you guidance as a child. Healthy parents provide consistent support and encourage you to have confidence in yourself. Dysfunctional parents are unable to do this. Instead the parents pass on their unresolved fears. In a closed family system, this leaves you with no direct experience of the dangers about which your parents are so worried. As a result, you are never given a realistic view of the world or taught ways to cope with life. You are left only with a vague sense that the world is a fearful place.

Loyalty Debts

Family traditions can serve a valuable purpose. They allow a family to share customs and beliefs, which give the family its own identity and a sense of unity. In codependent homes, however, traditions can become stifling and oppressive. You may not be aware of these restrictive traditions until you begin to separate from your family as a teenager.

Ralph told me about his loyalty to the traditions in his family and how they affected him as an adolescent.

"I call it my *Coming of Age Fantasy*," he said. "I would imagine I was a young knight in the Middle Ages. My family of nobles owned a beautiful castle and rich farmlands that had been passed down from father to son through the generations. I knew that when I became a man, these would be mine. It was an honor and responsibility that I would have to live up to. My father would take me aside and say, 'Son, all this will be yours. I've preserved what my father did and built on that. Don't destroy what it has taken your family generations to create.'

"Now for reality," said Ralph. "My father really did take me aside and tell me, 'Don't destroy what it has taken your family generations to create.' Only there was no castle. No farmlands. In fact, I had no idea what he was talking about. At best, he seemed to be referring to a kind of family honor based on adherence to certain cultural or religious traditions. At worst, he was telling me to be fearful, inhibited and to kowtow to authority figures — all of which repelled me.

"But," Ralph added, "whatever he meant, I got the emotional charge behind it. Something vital and important had been placed in my hands. If I destroy it I will show I am an ungrateful and uncaring person. This left me feeling crippled. All I could think was I owed it to my parents not to destroy their world."

Ralph sensed that there was something more behind his father's words than he could understand. Ralph was experiencing the weight of his family's invisible loyalties. His father's vague concern for protecting the family was really a plea to preserve the dysfunctional family system so that Ralph's parents did not have to face the pain of their own pasts. Hidden in his father's plea was an unconscious threat that Ralph would be punished if he were disloyal to the family. Ralph reacted to his father's appeal for loyalty by feeling pressured to control himself in all areas of his life.

If you still live by invisible loyalties, you may find yourself behaving in a similar way and falling into the following self-destructive patterns:

- You restrict yourself to activities and choices within the compass of what you think your family would approve. You stay away from other activities, no matter how much they might appeal to you.
- At the other extreme you may be aware of your family's expectations, and you may rebel against them. This is just as much an emotional sacrifice as going along with family loyalties. Your ties to your family still keep you from acting from your true self.
- You make the decisions you want, but put an excessive amount of energy into rationalizing that your choices will not hurt your parents, no matter how upset they seem.
- Every time you make a choice that goes against your parents' wishes, you feel guilty or that you owe them something.

I could give endless examples of teenagers making these kinds of sacrifices because of the guilt they feel for opposing their parents over family loyalty issues.

Aaron's family was Jewish, and he knew he hurt his parents by taking up with a non-Jewish woman. He "made it up to them" by taking the pre-med curriculum in school even though he had no desire to study medicine.

Mary Beth routinely turned down skiing invitations from friends because she felt she did not deserve them after the nervousness she had caused her parents by going on a cross-country hiking trip.

Lynne found herself having difficulty painting artistically because it seemed inexplicably to aggravate her mother.

Eric stayed at a job he hated because its competitive nature gave him something to talk about with his ambitious father.

With therapy you can begin to uncover your invisible loyalties to your family. You may see the ways in which you protected your parents as a teenager, and may still protect them, by limiting yourself. With help you can begin a healthy psychological separation from your family system. You can make choices based on your needs, rather than trying to guess what your parents want.

Teenagers And Sexuality

Dysfunctional families are full of confusion and paranoia about the exploration of sexuality. Reaching puberty and developing one's sexual identity is challenging for most people but is particularly difficult for a teenager from a troubled home. You will usually have a history of sexual abuse, physical and/or emotional incest and shame about your body. You can be raised in a repressive atmosphere that stifles healthy self-expression and self-confidence. Sexuality is a natural expression of life energy. To be energetic, outgoing and fully alive — and therefore, to be sexual — can be a threat to your family system.

By simply maturing physically, you can threaten your parents with abandonment. If your parents are enmeshed with you, they may want you to remain dependent on them. They can feel betrayed as your body changes and you grow into an adult.

If you are raised in a dysfunctional family, you learn to feel guilty when you experience pleasure. You can believe that being sexual is self-indulgent and even "dirty." Often without being told, you catch on that masturbation is something "bad" people do. These messages are common in our addictive society.

Because of your childhood experience, you may also fear pleasure. You can be caught in chronic shock. Your body can be locked up with repressed emotion and tension. You may be so rigid because of your mental and physical defenses, that the surrender of control necessary for sexual pleasure can be frightening.

Many co-dependents associate sexual intimacy with abuse. If you grew up having your personal boundaries violated by your family, it is natural to fear that your boundaries will not be respected by people in the present. It is also common to feel that you do not deserve to have such boundaries because they were taken away so early.

Sexual abuse strikes to your core very deeply. When you are sexually abused, especially by a parent or someone on whom you depend, you are usually left with a deep sense of betrayal and of being used.

One of the most common, yet most subtle, forms of sexual abuse is *emotional incest*. This is an extension of the way in which parents ask their children to take care of the parents' needs.

According to John Bradshaw,

> "It is very common for one or both parents in a dysfunctional marriage to bond inappropriately with one of their children . . . This relationship can easily become sexualized and romanticized. The daughter may become Daddy's Little Princess, or the son may become Mom's Little Man. In both cases the child is being abandoned. The parent is getting his needs met at the expense of the child's needs. The child needs a parent not a spouse."
>
> *Bradshaw On: The Family*

One of my clients, Roger, was unable to have a full sexual experience with his partner. As a child, he had been his mother's Little Man. She had emotionally incested Roger by making him her special favorite child. When Roger grew up and started to date women, he was able to have some kind of sexual involvement, but he would eventually shut down.

In therapy he began to see that by repressing his sexuality, he unconsciously kept himself from leaving his mother. As long as he could not have a satisfying sexual relationship with a woman, he didn't have to let go of his role as his mother's Little Husband. His struggle was compounded because he had repressed memories of physical incest that began to emerge as he felt safer in therapy and in his life in general. Interestingly Roger had not spoken with his mother for two or three years but was still controlled by her.

In therapy, Estelle worked through the emotional incest by her father. She got out her anger, terror and shame, as well as her tremendous love and caring for her father. She spoke to an empty chair as though her father were there. She told him that she was now going to go on, to have a life of her own and to have a relationship with a man. She said she was no longer his Little Girl and although she hated what he had done to her, she would always love him because he was her father. However, Estelle chose not to be around her father for more than a few hours once or twice a year because he still treated her as though she were his wife, instead of his daughter. By working in therapy and setting this boundary, Estelle was able to forgive her father for the past. She continued to let go of him, instead of waiting for him to change.

You Are Not To Blame

It is important to understand that as a child you are not responsible in any way for being abused — whether it is physical, sexual or emotional. Some people claim that sexual abuse feels good to the child. As a child, your body responds involuntarily to sexual stimulation, but that does not mean you want to have sex with your parent. Your body is simply stimulated to have a reaction. The offender may have told you that it felt good and you believed it.

"It's because of you that I'm doing this, because you like it so much."

You might start to think that is true because you are so easily influenced by your parents. Even if you had sexual feelings for your parents, which is common for a child, that does not mean you were responsible in any way for their actions. The parent is the one who has the power.

When you do not receive healthy affection as a child, you might begin to associate abuse with love. For instance, when you are emotionally incested, you can mistake your parent's incestuous attention for healthy love and the special feeling it gives you. This can skew your thinking about love and interfere with your intimate relationships as an adult. You can develop a pseudo-intimacy with your parents that you seek to replicate in your adult relationships. Until you heal from your emotional incest, you will probably remain confused about healthy love.

Even if you convince yourself that as a child you liked being abused by a parent, you are still not to blame for what was done to you. The truth is when you are abused in any way as a child, you are powerless and have no choice in the situation.

Abuse is never the fault of the child. You are not responsible for what your parents and other adults do to you. They are the adults. You are the child.

If you were a child victim of sexual abuse or emotional incest remember, anyone who tells you that you had a choice is wrong. You are probably living in an illusion of control if you think otherwise. This illusion may be appealing because if you can convince yourself that the abuse was your fault, you can avoid feeling the pain of your helplessness and vulnerability at the time. This is the deepest psychological pain there is. Feeling this initial pain and working through it, however, is the only way I have found to free yourself from its effects.

Abuse does not need to be confused with discipline. At every age there are appropriate ways to discipline a child. Clearly stated consequences that the child must face for a specific behavior is an effective method of discipline. Physical punishment, however, is not necessary and, as we will see, is a form of abuse. Any use of an implement for spanking, whether it is a wooden spoon, a tree branch or a hairbrush, is inappropriate.

Understanding the difference between discipline and abuse is important if you are a parent. If you have hurt your children, it is appropriate to feel a healthy guilt for your abusive behavior, to hold yourself accountable and to make amends to your children. This will help your recovery and model responsible behavior for your children.

The Many Faces Of Abuse

Although our addictive society denies that many behaviors are abusive, a child can be damaged in a number of ways. The following list can help you to better understand the nature of abuse:

- **Physical abuse** can be anything from a slap on the knee to punching and kicking. Any time someone crosses your physical boundaries without your consent, they are abusing you.
- **Psychological abuse** can be just as damaging as physical abuse. In some cases it can be more harmful. Psychological abuse, also referred to as emotional abuse, can be very subtle. If someone talks to you abusively, uses sarcasm or criticizes you destructively, that is abusive.
- **Sexual abuse** is any physical or emotional attack that relates to your sexuality. Rape, physical or emotional incest, voyeurism, invasion of privacy and inappropriate sexual comments are all sexually abusive. There is a wide range of sexual abuse. For example, a slap on your mouth is a sexual attack because your mouth is an important part of your sexuality.
- **Gender abuse** is any put-down of a certain gender. The attack can be a general criticism of males or females. Such attacks can leave a child feeling ashamed for his or her sex, which is a central part of a child's identity.
- **Intellectual abuse** is very common in dysfunctional homes. It is any disregard for your thoughts, opinions and ideas. When you are not allowed to think freely and make mistakes along the way, your intellect is stifled. Many co-dependents who are naturally very bright grow up thinking they are not intelligent due to this kind of abuse. Many learning disabilities and problems in school can be traced to intellectual abuse in the home.

- **Neglect** is another form of abuse. As much as you are affected by what happens in your home, you are also affected by what does *not* happen. If your parents intentionally or unintentionally deprive you of emotional support, you will be deeply wounded. Parents can also deprive a child through isolation. For instance, you can be left in your room crying with no one to comfort you. You can also be emotionally isolated by "violent silence." This is when parents punish you by saying only a minimum of terse words. Your reaction to this kind of trauma can be just as strong as your reaction to more obvious abuse.

- **Witnessing abuse** is as damaging to you as being attacked directly. This applies to any of the above forms of abuse. When you watch a sibling or a parent being abused, you feel powerless, and you live with a sense that your turn could come at any time. This can be terrifying for a child.

- **Spiritual abuse** covers all of the above. It is anything that causes you to protect yourself, physically, mentally, emotionally and sexually. Any time someone does something that makes it unsafe for you to be fully present and to keep your heart and spirit fully open, they are acting abusively. To develop as a spiritual person, a child needs love, support and safety. It is your birthright for your inner spirit to be free and to fully express itself in the world.

It can be very important to your recovery to be clear about what behaviors are damaging to you and to others. As you learn about the nature of abuse, you can begin to uncover what was done to you as a child, and you can take steps to make your life free of abuse in the present.

Medicating The Pain

Using something to distract you from the abuse and pain of your dysfunctional family is a behavior that seems to come naturally to human beings. Starting when you are very young, you can be tempted to do many things to your body and your mind to turn off the pain. Children often retreat into a fantasy world. They create places and characters that help them to forget the painful realities of their lives or that give their sufferings a heroic or noble dimension. As a pre-teen and a teenager, it is very common to turn to some form of numbing or medication to escape from reality.

In her tape, *Co-dependency: The Trap and the Triumph*, Sharon Wegscheider-Cruse identifies the four most common methods of medicating your pain as:

- Drugs and alcohol
- Nicotine
- Eating disorders (anorexia, bulimia, overeating, sugar addiction)
- Relationships

When you are a teenager, you usually can find little help for these problems. You may step outside of your family system only to discover that in our society blocking out the world and medicating inner discomfort through addictive substances and processes is widely accepted.

In her book, *Escape From Intimacy*, Anne Wilson Schaef distinguishes between *substance addictions* and *process addictions*. The substances include alcohol, illegal and prescription drugs, nicotine, caffeine and food. Her list of process addictions includes work, sports, the accumulation of money or possessions, spending money, gambling, exercise, religion, worry, television, constant activity and more.

Anything can become an addiction. As a teenager you have the opportunity and the encouragement to start smoking, drinking, drugging or developing some kind of obsession or compulsion. You may even develop an obsession with school that is a precursor of workaholism.

In fact, schoolwork and an obsession with academic achievement is often a socially approved "drug" for ignoring emotional problems. Performing well academically can delude you and your parents into thinking that you are emotionally healthy.

Academic pressure and competition can also be used as an explanation for your distress as a teenager. Parents and school officials may focus attention on scholastic performance instead of exploring your emotional needs or the family's dysfunction. This is unfortunate, because there is a clear link between problems in school and problems at home. As Bob Earll explains,

> "Adult children from alcoholic and dysfunctional families often suffer from a learning impairment. After all the yelling, screaming, beatings, mixed messages, lies, triangulation (communication through third parties) and absence of approval, it's no wonder many of us have a hard time focusing and retaining information that is being presented to us. *It's okay if something has to be demonstrated 10 times before you understand it. It takes what it takes."*

I Got Tired Of Pretending

By ignoring your emotional life and focusing solely on academic progress, our education system reinforces the co-dependent behavior of your home. In this way, attending school enables you to delay facing up to the truth about yourself and your family until you graduate from high school, college or graduate school. If you eventually get help for your co-dependency, you can seek out guidance on an emotional, psychological and spiritual level to develop those parts of yourself that never received an education.

Teen Pregnancy

As a young woman you have another way to escape from the pain of your dysfunctional home. You may try to take care of your emotional needs and alleviate your anxiety by having a child. If you become pregnant, you may want to keep your child because you feel the child will be the only person who really loves you. At a young age you can easily pass on the disease of co-dependency to the next generation by having a child to fulfill your emotional needs.

Running Away From Home

You may also run away from home to escape the enmeshment or abuse of your dysfunctional family, but the shadow of your home can follow you. As you get your feet on the ground away from your family, you may find that your ability to love has been damaged. You can become depressed and feel the pull of the obligation to take care of your parents.

You may fight this invisible loyalty by being resentful and abusive towards your parents. You may criticize your parents and live a lifestyle of anti-conformity. You may seek to frighten your parents by telling them you live a dangerous, unhealthy life. As we have seen, when you behave in these ways towards your parents, your life is being affected by invisible loyalties, just as much as when you act in the ways your parents expect. If you tend towards either extreme, you do not live from your true self.

Parents who are co-dependent but are basically good loving people can be hurt by these harmful ways of establishing your own identity. If you can begin to heal from your past, you can differentiate from your parents without acting out of your co-dependency and causing them needless pain.

You Can't Run From Yourself

"Even 3,000 miles was not enough!"

So said Valerie, a young woman who left home in her teens and deliberately moved across the country to be far away from her family. It did not work. She still felt attached, and the emotional problems she thought she would leave behind migrated with her.

If you are co-dependent, it is not unusual for you to leave home and fail in the outside world. You may return home, feeling as though you are crazy, just as you had always feared. You may not see the connection between your struggle to establish yourself in the world and your loyalty to your dysfunctional family.

In *After The Tears*, the authors quote young people who returned to live with their troubled parents. The authors write,

> "When asked why they moved back home, they focus on their subjective failure at school or in jobs . . . When asked,

'What do you think would happen if you and your sisters or brothers moved out of the home?' First comes surprise at the question, then the fears, 'They'd divorce. Dad would beat Mom. They'd die. They'd go crazy. My dad would lose his job . . . the outside world would invade them if we weren't there to protect them.' "

Middelton-Moz and Dwinell

Your co-dependency can exert a powerful pull on you to stay enmeshed with your parents and to try to save the family system. Until you seek treatment for your addictions and your underlying disease of co-dependency, you will not be able to take responsibility for yourself in the way that is possible for a young adult. It is never too early to find 12-Step programs and counseling with a therapist who is knowledgeable about co-dependency.

With help you can begin to be independent from your parents. You can learn to acknowledge your parents' pain and realize there are limits to what you can do about it. You can let your parents grow from their pain. If your parents seek help for themselves, you can learn to be supportive towards them as they take the steps they need to heal from their pasts. As you do this, you may find that you can stand on your own in the world and still be loving to the people in your life.

Some Things To Do: A Letter To Your Parents

As you did at the end of the second chapter, find a safe, quiet place. Go inside again and connect with yourself as a teenager. If you can, ask through prayer for the Universe, God/Goddess, to help you to have a memory of a time when you were angry at one of your parents.

Try not to judge yourself for feeling angry. Anger isn't good or bad, it just is. If you are angry about a situation, it is important to honor that.

Write a letter from your teenager to the parent. You do not need to send the letter. It is for you.

Allow your teenager to write freely about how he or she experienced the event and how he or she felt about it. Be sure to include "I" statements such as, "I'm angry that

_____ ."

Write until you feel complete. Then check in with yourself. Notice what's going on with you and how your body feels. Affirm yourself for having the courage to express your anger in a clear way.

When you are done, try to remember a time you were angry at your other parent. Now write a letter to that parent and see how you feel.

4

Romancing The Inner Child

Three young women, Jeanine, Eileen and Marcie, all had troubled childhoods. Jeanine's father had died when she was four years old. Her mother had remarried and was more comfortable with her new husband and their two children than she was with Jeanine. Eileen's father was an untreated alcoholic and compulsive gambler, and her mother held the family together despite her husband's verbal abuse. Marcie had been sexually abused by an uncle when she was 11.

The three women went out for a drive on a Saturday afternoon, just intending to go to the malls and maybe see a movie. None of them talked much about the past. They talked about "boys" and about their relationships. Jeanine had a date that night with her boyfriend, Bill, so they had to watch their time. Jeanine had been spending a lot less time with her two friends since meeting Bill.

Jeanine had a lot to say about Bill. He was almost 20 years older than her. She felt extremely attached to him, but they often fought. He was addicted to TV, hunting, fishing and sailing, as well as any spectator sport he could attend. This left little time for them to spend together. However, when Jeanine thought about leaving Bill, she panicked. Because of her father's death and her mother's shift of loyalties, Jeanine had a tremendous fear of being abandoned. She did not realize that her reluctance to leave an unsatisfying relationship stemmed from her troubled childhood.

As Jeanine complained about Bill, her friends nodded in understanding. Eileen was sympathetic, partly to cover her feelings of resentment. A part of Eileen wanted Jeanine and Bill to break up, so that Jeanine would be alone like her. She told herself that wasn't very nice and she tried to be more sympathetic to Jeanine.

"Of course, you can't expect someone to be perfect," Eileen said. "I mean, he does give you nice gifts. And at least you have someone."

Eileen had spent years watching her mother put up with neglect and abuse from her father. To tolerate such behavior was the norm for her.

Marcie was less sympathetic. Her recent breakup with her boyfriend, Stan, was one in a long series of futile "love affairs" that left her bitter about the possibility of ever having a lasting relationship. She felt that sooner or later any man would show his true colors and damage her sense of herself.

She bitterly expressed her feelings, telling Jeanine, "Get rid of him. You don't need him anyway." It was easier for Marcie to act tough than to admit that she was lonely and discouraged.

As Jeanine listened to the different advice of her friends, she grew more fearful of losing Bill, of never having a fulfilling relationship. Jeanine longed for someone with whom she could share these feelings. She was afraid to be more vulnerable with her friends, and she had no one at home to talk to. Her mother had never been receptive to hearing Jeanine's feelings and disapproved of Bill because of his age.

Instead of sharing further with Eileen and Marcie, Jeanine turned the conversation to Eileen. Hadn't she met a guy she liked? Harold? What had happened with that?

Eileen turned red. It was true, she and Harold had gone out and she had liked him. But she wasn't going to let herself get sucked into anything until she was sure Harold was not like her father. She was so cautious that she didn't let herself be spontaneous with him. She even had trouble thinking of things to talk about. She was paralyzed by fear. The more she liked him the more she withdrew emotionally, until he lost interest.

To her friends Eileen simply said, "We went out but we just weren't very compatible."

Eileen knew that this wasn't accurate but it was the best she could do. She was afraid that she would become depressed if she told her friends about her tremendous fear of men.

Marcie shrugged and said caustically, "It's all just a big no-win game."

When Marcie first met someone, her hopes flared and she fell head over heels in love. She told herself this time would be different. She and her lover would immediately become intensely involved. Marcie threw herself completely into the relationship. But a part of her held her breath, waiting for the inevitable. It usually came a few months later. She began to see things about her lover that she didn't like. He would pull back and be less intense. She didn't want to give him a chance to dump her, so she dumped him first. Sometimes the man would call for weeks afterwards, begging for a chance to talk about it, to make up for whatever he might have done, to get back together. She would not talk to him or explain her behavior. When it was over there was no going back, and she had probably already attracted someone new.

The three young women drove on in silence. A sense of the impossibility of a "decent" relationship filled their minds and hearts. They hoped and they dreamed, but they always seemed to end up disillusioned. There didn't seem much point in asking why.

In this chapter we will look at the problems you may
have with intimacy if you are co-dependent. We have seen
how you repress your feelings, develop distorted thinking
and lose touch with your true self when you take care of
your parents as a child. We have seen that you are susceptible to addictions if you are co-dependent. If you do
not seek treatment, these patterns can deeply affect your
ability to form healthy relationships and to experience
love as an adult. Like Jeanine, Marcie and Eileen, you may
live in a world in which intimate relationships always
seem to fail or become dissatisfying. You may wonder
why you end up in relationships that turn out to be
similar to the unhealthy relationships of your childhood.
You may struggle through these relationships without
seeing the connection between your present discontent
and your dysfunctional childhood.

This may be a difficult chapter for you to read. Falling
in love can be so joyful and beautiful. It is a time when
your body sings, your heart overflows and your hopes
shine like stars. Co-dependency and addictions can rob
you of this joy. They can reduce falling in love to a short-
lived false high, followed by the familiar destructive patterns of your past from which you were trying to escape.

Take heart, though. There is a way out. As you heal the
issues from your family of origin, you can eventually free
yourself from repeating the kinds of relationships you experienced as a child. You can free yourself from addiction,
gain a clear sense of yourself, open your heart to people in
the present and experience lasting love and intimacy.

The Void

To begin to free yourself you need to understand the
unconscious attractions that can pull you into dysfunctional relationships. To get to the root of these attractions,
it is necessary to look back to your childhood.

As a child raised in an unhealthy family, you learn to
abandon yourself to take care of the family system. If you

remain cut off from yourself and do not heal from your past, you can live with what many co-dependents call an "inner void" or a "hole inside." This is the stress you carry from your childhood that was never relieved by proper caring from your parents.

As Pia Mellody explains in her book *Facing Co-dependence*, if you grow up in a functional family, your parents are alert to your neediness. When you are under stress, you will cry and your parents will come and reduce the stress. Your parents honor your feelings and do what they can to meet your needs. You learn that you will be regarded by your parents. This gives you a sense of connection and self-worth.

When this does not happen, you are emotionally (and often physically) abandoned. You are not regarded and your needs are not met. The stress from being neglected teaches you that you do not matter. You do not gain a sense of personal worth or power. You learn to look to other people and external things to reduce this stress, to give you a sense of self-worth.

Through The Eyes Of A Child

While many co-dependents are aware of an inner longing, they often do not connect it with the neglect of their childhoods. As a child you are not able to perceive clearly that the relationship between you and your parents is unhealthy. You depend on your parents for survival and for self-validation. It would be too frightening to acknowledge that your parents are sick and unable to take care of you in the ways that you need. From your point of view as a child if your parents cannot take care of you, you believe you will die.

It is natural for any child to idealize his or her parents. As a child your parents are larger than life. In your eyes, they appear almost god-like. In a healthy family as you grow older you lose this child's perspective and learn to see your parents more realistically.

The Myth Of The Perfect Parent

If you were raised in a dysfunctional family, however, you may unconsciously idealize your parents and cling to an image of them as all-knowing, infallible beings. In spite of the troubles in your family, you can convince yourself that you had a deep, safe, nurturing connection with your parents. In your mind you create a pseudo-bonding, or what Robert Firestone calls a *fantasy bond*. This fantasy keeps you from grieving for the true bonding you did not get if your parents were co-dependent/addicted.

To preserve your belief in a deep connection between you and your parents, you minimize experiences that challenge your illusory view of your parents and amplify positive memories of your parents. This remaking of reality is called *sincere delusion*. This is a human defense mechanism, similar to chronic shock, that protects you from experiencing more than you can tolerate. In sincere delusion you truly believe the idealized image you create of your parents. You literally don't see your parents' shortcomings and the neglect or even abuse you suffered at their hands.

This is not to say that you did not develop a meaningful connection with your parents or experience moments when you felt the love between you. Almost any connection you had, even if it was only when you were very young, can be very important to you later in your life. It can be healing for you to cherish the loving memories from your childhood.

In most dysfunctional family systems, however, the emotional connection between parents and their children is usually damaged. You may have received nurturing but it may not have been consistent enough to give you the strong sense of self you need to function well as an adult. By creating a fantasy bond, you avoid grieving that you did not get the attention you needed. You can also keep from feeling the loss of any deep bonding which was later severed by the problems in your family.

Just You, Me . . . And Addiction

As long as you hold on to your fantasy bond with your parents, you keep from acknowledging the source of your inner emptiness. Instead of healing this inner void through a gradual grieving process, you will do what you can to fill your emptiness in the present. This desperate search can easily lead you into addiction.

Co-dependents are characterized by an underlying addictive process. If you are co-dependent, you can become addicted to anything that promises to take away your pain (reality that is intolerable). Essentially you believe your addiction will put you back in time to the ideal nurturing and safety you believe you once had. As Bradshaw says, "In all compulsive/addictive behavior the illusion of connection is restored" *(Bradshaw On: The Family)*.

Many co-dependents suffer from addictions related to intimacy. These addictions are sexual addiction, romance addiction and love addiction (also referred to as relationship addiction). Although we will discuss these addictions separately and in their most obvious forms, most co-dependents carry pieces of all of these addictions within them and suffer from them to varying degrees.

As with many addictions, addiction to sex, romance and love originate in dysfunctional families and are reinforced by schools, churches, the media and all the other institutions of society. Because they are accepted and encouraged by society they are difficult to weed out. However, as with all addictions, they need to be identified and made conscious in order to be healed.

Sexual Addiction

A sex addict is obsessed with sex and escapes from reality through pornography, masturbation, extramarital affairs, voyeurism, exhibitionism and, in the severest cases, rape and incest. Our society encourages sexual addiction in many ways. Our taboos and distorted thinking can stifle healthy sexual expression. This is particularly true in many

religions. To the opposite extreme, advertisements, the
media and the entertainment industry objectify men and
women, often emphasizing sex above all else.

The connection between addictive behavior and the
search for the fantasy bond can probably be seen most
clearly in sexual addiction. Sexual pleasure may be the
closest you can come to recapturing the bliss and comfort
most infants feel with their mothers. Sexual pleasure can
be an enriching and fulfilling experience when you allow
yourself to sink into these blissful feelings and integrate
them into your life.

If you are an addict, however, you never feel satisfied.
As with any addiction, the pleasurable feelings do not take
away for long the stress you feel from the inconsistent
nurturing you received as a child. Instead of accepting
this, you look to sexual experiences to give you the deep
connection you believe you had with your parents.

Being sexual with your partner is an important piece of
intimate sharing. Sex without this connection, however,
can leave you feeling empty and unfulfilled. Our addictive
materialistic society puts so much emphasis on pursuing
someone. The problem is that people do not know what
to do once they "have" the person. When you act from
addiction, you do not appreciate what is in the moment. It
is never enough. As you free yourself from addiction, you
can learn to fully enjoy and honor another person.

The goal of recovery from sexual addiction is to enjoy
your sexuality in the ways you choose, instead of being
controlled by your addiction. If you and your partner
work to free yourselves from addiction and from your
underlying co-dependency, you can nurture the spiritual
passion that is possible between two committed lovers. In
healthy marriages and relationships the partners maintain
a deep mutual love and, from time to time, rekindle that
special "in-love" feeling. This is a spiritual connection that
runs deeper than the initial thrill of falling in love.

In her book, *Coupleship*, Sharon Wegscheider-Cruse defines spiritual as, "full of life, full of passion, full of
energy." When you live spiritually, you can feel a joy and

an excitement about being alive. This feeling can lay dormant for years, smothered by the pain and struggles of a dysfunctional family. When two individuals bring their spiritual energy together, they can have a vital, passionate relationship. In this context physical sharing can be a joyful experience.

You may find that physical sharing not only brings back the bliss of your early infant days with your mother, but it also reawakens your deep feelings of fear and anger towards her, especially if she was co-dependent and addicted. If you can be aware of these feelings and work with your partner as you heal them, you can enjoy your sexuality in the present while you free yourself from your past.

As you continue to mourn the holding and physical nurturing you did not get on a consistent basis, you can become more comfortable with physical sharing. Instead of turning to addiction to avoid intimacy, you can begin to honor your need for closeness and to experience the joy of a passionate spiritual sexual relationship.

For more information and an excellent discussion of sexual addiction, I suggest you read *Out of the Shadows* by Patrick Carnes.

Romance Addiction

According to Anne Wilson Schaef in her book, *Escape From Intimacy,* "The romance addict is in love with the *idea* of romance."

When you are addicted to romance, you turn to fantasy to fill your inner emptiness. You piece together this fantasy from popular movies, novels and songs. As you spend more time in fantasy, you can become further removed from reality. If your addiction progresses, you can have affairs, liaisons and even multiple marriages. At the severest levels you will seek romantic liaisons that endanger your life.

If you are addicted to romance, you may become involved romantically with someone while remaining emotionally unavailable by living in your illusion. You can go through the motions of a relationship, but keep your feelings and fantasies from the other person. Often you may even be afraid of relationships and sex. After a short affair, the romantic allure begins to wear off. To maintain your illusions, you move on to someone new. You can thrive on excitement, chaos and staying one step ahead. As long as you keep moving, you feel "alive." You can avoid taking responsibility for your actions.

According to Schaef, if you are a romance addict, you can feel safe with fantasies and affairs because you can fulfill certain needs without having to acknowledge your true needs. You never have to risk having your deepest needs rejected. You can insulate yourself from what you believe to be the harsh reality of the world. As long as you live in fantasy, you can feel safe and innocent. This is a strong lure to stay addicted.

As with alcoholics or chemically dependent people, you can be "drugged" by romance addiction. Over time your mind becomes affected from distorting reality. And as you become further removed from being able to connect with others in meaningful ways, your pain and inner emptiness increases.

The church, with its emphasis on purity and its focus on a life beyond this one, can support your escape into romance. Schools, which glorify sports heroes and prom queens, and popular songs and movies that idealize love at first sight, reinforce society's message that romantic addiction is acceptable.

While you may not carry romance addiction to its extreme, you may suffer from its effects to some degree.

To look for signs of romance addiction in yourself, you may want to ask yourself:

- At times do you escape into romantic fantasies to avoid being vulnerable with your partner?
- How much emphasis do you place on romantic gestures?
- Do you believe a conflict should be resolved if you bring your partner a gift?

• Do you expect that somehow your relationship will eventually take on the mystery and adventure of the romances you see in the movies or read about in novels?

It is healthy to want romance in a relationship. Romance only becomes a problem when you give it too much importance. As you weed out traces of your romance addiction, it can be helpful if you remember that romance is the icing, not the cake.

Love Addiction

In some ways because it is so widespread, love addiction or relationship addiction, can be harder to identify than the other addictions we have discussed. Although we will discuss this addiction primarily in regard to romantic relationships, there can be an element of addiction in any relationship because of the co-dependent character of our society.

Co-dependent Matchmaking

Although the fantasy bond helps you survive in a dysfunctional home, it outlives its usefulness. It stays with you into adulthood where it can lead you into addiction. Along with sexual addiction and romance addiction, your longing for parental love can lead you to become compulsively attached to relationships.

Co-dependency exists on a continuum: it is possible to suffer from many degrees of the disease. Using Bowen's scale of self-differentiation as a guide, you can get a sense of the extent of your own co-dependency. For instance, if you have a strong sense of yourself and you are able to honor your emotions without letting them control you, you probably suffer very little from co-dependency.

As Bowen points out the level of your self-differentiation usually influences your choice of partners. For instance, in most cases a person with a strong sense of self

and clear personal boundaries will not choose to be intimate with a severely co-dependent person. However, if
you are extremely co-dependent and have a low level of
self-differentiation, you will most likely be attracted to
someone who also has a poor sense of his or her identity.
In this way you end up with someone with whom you can
replicate the co-dependent relationships of your childhood.

If you have a low level of self-differentiation, your
longing for the fantasy bond probably lies beneath your
attraction. On an unconscious level you may believe that,
if you could just do it over again with your parents, you
could regain the all-nurturing deep bonding you imagine
you had with them.

Since it is not possible to go back in time you do the next
best thing: you find someone who is similar to your parents. Unfortunately, this means instead of finding a healthy
partner who can give you love in the present, you find
someone who is as emotionally unavailable to you as your
parents were. You keep coming back to the same dry well.

As you learned as a child, you give your personal power
to another person. Even in the face of painful reality you
continue to hope that your partner will provide you with
unconditional and constant regard.

These unconscious motivations can be subtle and powerful. Kim told me, "I knew there were problems in my
family. I used to tell my friends that I'd never marry
anyone like my parents. I could even point out exactly
where they went wrong. In spite of this I kept ending up
with men who were identical to my father. I couldn't
figure it out." Kim eventually began to see that she had
been drawn to enmeshment with another co-dependent
person, rather than to healthy love.

Enmeshed Love

When you first fall into *enmeshed love* you may see the
similarity between you and your partner as a sign of com-
patibility and mutual understanding. You confuse meeting a

kindred spirit with falling in love. You believe that the "miracle of love" will wash away the pain of your past. This sets you up to become addicted to your partner.

When you become addicted to another person you go through an addictive cycle similar to that of other addictions. You start out at the heights of ecstasy. You go through what I call an enmeshment high, believing that this relationship will finally make you feel whole.

This illusive state of enmeshed love can be very alluring. You may believe that you have finally found the right person and that anything is possible. You will be totally accepted and totally accepting. There will be no need for learning relationship skills or for resolving conflicts.

When the reality of the relationship begins to show through, you fall from your false high. You begin to see that your partner is not an omnipotent parent but simply another human being. Your partner's own co-dependency starts to show through. Once again, you find yourself in a relationship with someone similar to your parents who is emotionally unavailable.

"I Can't Live With Or Without You"

When your partner is not emotionally open to you or pushes you away in more obvious ways, you can swing from ecstasy to despair. This is the other side of the enmeshment high. If you are co-dependent, instead of walking away and finding a healthy partner, you may slip into addiction. You become obsessed with your partner. You may turn against or reject the person or you may do whatever you can to keep your partner from leaving.

If your partner does not leave, you feel temporary relief from your compulsion to fill your inner void, until the next time he or she withdraws or disregards you. If your efforts do not work and your partner leaves you, you remain in despair until you find another person over whom to become ecstatic. You may even turn to other addictions until you meet a new partner. You then start the addictive cycle over again. You do not take time to heal when a relation-

ship ends because you are too obsessed with finding
another partner. When you are caught in addiction, you
lose sight of your relationship as an ongoing process between you and another person. You tend to see the relationship as something to possess. You become obsessed
with needing to be with your partner and you feel jealous
and rejected when he or she needs time alone or with
others. In some cases you may resort to dishonesty, in-
trigue and desperate efforts to control your partner.

"We Had It All"

In your desperation to keep from letting go of a relationship, you conveniently forget anything that indicates
the relationship is bad for you. Just as you delude yourself
that you had a deep bonding with your parents, you can
convince yourself that you had a perfect relationship with
your partner. This is called *euphoric recall*. You remember
the special moments of your relationship, especially the
initial enmeshment high, and forget the painful and abusive times. You convince yourself that some day you will
be able to get "it" back — the glow, the passion, the
ecstasy. You continue to abandon yourself for an illusion.

Giving All For Security

If you are addicted to relationships, you can pay a high
price for holding on to a partner at all costs. To avoid
being alone you may stay in an abusive and unfulfilling
relationship that keeps you removed from yourself.

When you stay with a person out of addiction, you can
find yourself in what Sharon Wegscheider-Cruse calls a
spiritually dead relationship (Coupleship). This is a relationship
in which there is no real intimacy and no real sharing.
You and your partner may not resolve issues that
threaten the relationship. You may not acknowledge the
problems in your sex life. You swallow resentments.
Security, which fills an important need in healthy relationships, becomes everything. You are willing to sacrifice
love, intimacy, growth and happiness to avoid being alone.

The relationship can serve as a bandage to cover the wounds of your hurtful past.

"I've Been Here Before"

In your effort to maintain a spiritually dead relationship, you may turn to the survival skills you learned in your dysfunctional home. You may believe if you could just behave correctly, you could "fix" your partner and get the love you want. You can reenact your childhood by trying to follow rigid rules, keep secrets and remain loyal to your partner at all costs. If you are caught in a childhood pattern of trying to fix your partner, you will have little chance for intimacy.

When you try to fix the relationship, you are preserving a facade of closeness instead of learning healthy ways to truly connect with your partner. You may appear to have excellent communication skills but beneath the facade you feel lost when it comes to connecting deeply with another person. These skills can make it more difficult for you to recognize your addiction because you can appear adept at relating to others.

A Co-dependent Love Affair

Jill's story of how she met, fell in love with and married Ed illustrates the way love addiction can lure you to an unhealthy partner and lead you to try to preserve the relationship at your own expense.

Jill was a warm, caring person with a painful past that she sought to transcend. Jill's mother had been trapped in the role of the caretaker of the family. She was expected to be the strong one in the family and to do everything for her husband and daughter. She resented her position and took her frustration out on Jill. Jill's father had been passive and dependent on his wife. Jill got more attention from him than she got from her mother. In Jill's eyes her father was a saint in comparison to her mother.

Jill told me, "When I left home, I thought if I could find someone similar to my father, I could have a happy marriage. I had always assumed my mother was the problem.

"When I met Ed, I thought he was the one. In the beginning, Ed appeared loving and willing to work anything out. I was in love. We seemed to see eye to eye on so much. We both wanted to be free of our abusive mothers and to build a healthy relationship. We were lost souls, orphans in the storm who found peace and understanding in each other's arms. We decided we were going to make the kind of life for ourselves that we felt we had never had as children. We had both survived painful neglect and the lack of real family warmth, closeness and openness. We were going to make up for what we had missed in the past through the strength of our relationship. It was us against the world."

What Jill and Ed experienced was an enmeshment high. Instead of coming together as two distinct individuals with mutual interests, their identities merged. For Jill and Ed this fusion seemed the most wonderfully satisfying emotional state imaginable. They needed nothing else. But was it healthy? And would it last?

For Jill and Ed the answer was no, it did not last. What began with such hope ended in romantic tragedy. Their relationship deteriorated into alcoholism, constant fights, psychological and occasionally physical abuse. After years of struggle, they finally divorced. Jill wondered what had happened. What had gone wrong? Did it have to be this way?

From True Love To Caretaking

After her divorce from Ed, Jill found out what had gone wrong. She started therapy and began to see that she and Ed had acted out the patterns from their childhoods. Instead of mutual love Jill had found an enmeshment, similar to her relationship with her parents, that drained her of her spirit.

"At first," said Jill, "we supported each other through our problems. We were fellow sufferers. But soon Ed's problems with his mother dominated our relationship. He started to direct the anger and mistrust he felt for his mother towards me. One night he got drunk and was verbally abusive to me. I was shocked. I had never seen this side of him. I told myself that his behavior was just an aberration, that everyone goes through ups and downs. I figured it just showed how much pain he was in and I tried to be more understanding.

"However, hearing the man I loved scream at me opened up a wound from my past. Just as I had blamed myself for my mother's neglect, I felt that I caused Ed's outburst by not being caring enough. Ed encouraged me in this by blaming me for his moods and his anger. When he did, I would become depressed and think, 'Maybe it's not even something I did. It could just be my personality. Maybe there's something fundamentally wrong with me.' I was terrified of his leaving me. I felt I had found the perfect partner and if he left, it would prove that I was unlovable."

To please Ed and to keep him from leaving her, Jill slipped into the self-destructive patterns of behavior she had learned as a child.

"By blaming myself I was able to excuse Ed's abusive behavior. If I started to have feelings, I would intellectualize them and figure out why I shouldn't feel that way. I didn't want to upset him by showing my feelings. I was especially careful to suppress my anger because I thought it was unjustified and I was afraid of how he would respond. Soon I was taking care of him by suppressing myself so that I wouldn't bother him in any way.

"I also took responsibility for his sick behavior by agreeing to be the one with the problem. We both were drinking too much, but he insisted he was in control and I was the one who couldn't handle alcohol. Ironically as his drinking worsened and he became irresponsible, I took on more domestic responsibility. I took care of the bills, the yard work and the car. After all, I reasoned, Ed worked so hard.

"This was a familiar role for me. My mother had always blamed me for her problems. My entire childhood I tried to please her by being super-responsible. It never seemed to work, but I ended up doing the same thing in my marriage with Ed."

With only the best intentions, Jill was caught by her past. Her upbringing had conditioned her to go beyond her limits in giving to others. What began as compassion and love slipped into co-dependency and addiction.

False Comfort

One of the payoffs for staying in an unhealthy relationship is that it is familiar. In fact, you may not know that there is anything better because you have had little or no experience with someone being there for you or meeting your needs. Even if a relationship is painful, you may find a peculiar safety and comfort living in an atmosphere like that of your childhood. You have been through it before so you know what to expect. To change is threatening because it means trying new ways of living that were unsafe to explore as you grew up.

It is also more comfortable to stay in a dysfunctional relationship because our society still teaches us that we are more valuable in a relationship than we are alone.

Doreen's experience reveals how society condones relationship addiction.

"As far back as I can remember," Doreen said, "I've had a best friend. My school encouraged this with a 'buddy system' and by working in pairs in class. I have very few memories of my childhood that do not include one of my successive best friends.

"When I met Phil, he became my new best friend. We were married very young. Within a year I was unhappy in the marriage and sought help from a minister. I found that the church preferred me to be in an unhealthy relationship rather than alone. I even got the same message from my friends. As far as I could tell, everyone thought the security of a relationship was more important than my happiness."

Unfortunately, in the long run, this precarious comfort can be very damaging to you. According to Schaef,

"The stress of sick relationships can be fatal; some forms of illness appear to be related to the stress of staying in a dead or sick relationship. Many people directly trace their cancer, for example, to their relationship addiction . . . "

Escape From Intimacy

Freedom From Addiction

Although you may turn to an addiction to escape the pain of your past, it is only a matter of time before the pain your addiction causes begins to outweigh the pain it covers up. You may feel the most pain when your addictions begin to interfere with your relationships. It is at this point that many co-dependents seek help for their addictions.

As Joseph Cruse says,

"One of the driving forces in the commitment to recovery from any addiction is a hope for a spiritual and meaningful relationship with a special person. Additional motivation is received from wanting to improve one's relationship with all those persons in one's life — family members, social acquaintances, friends and co-workers."

Focus Magazine *(June/July 1988)*

An important step you can take to heal from an addiction is to accept that it is damaging your life. The First Step of the 12 Steps of Alcoholics Anonymous can help you to do this. ("We admitted we were powerless over alcohol — that our lives had become unmanageable." You can simply replace the word alcohol with any addiction.) It is a paradox but when you own your addiction and acknowledge that it is controlling you, you free yourself to begin to heal from your addiction.

With supportive friends, 12-Step support groups and a therapist who is knowledgeable in addictions, you can be loving to yourself as you heal. You can feel empowered as you take responsibility, but not blame, for your addiction. You can reclaim your power to choose, instead of being driven compulsively by addiction.

Breaking The Addictive Cycle

As you become clearer about your addictions you can learn to intervene in the cycle of your addictions. The addictive cycle is similar for any addiction. We will continue to focus on love addiction and look at how you can free yourself from its grip.

To begin to arrest your love addiction, you learn to stop yourself before you act out of compulsion. When your partner physically or emotionally withdraws, you feel an addictive urge to react by rejecting your partner or doing whatever you can to keep him or her from leaving.

As you become more aware of the addictive cycle when your partner pulls away, you can stop, be sure to breathe deeply, feel the emotions that may surface and keep from speaking or acting compulsively. After you do this, you may want to call a friend for support, take a walk or do something to support yourself. As you gradually learn not to abandon yourself to addiction, your self-esteem will rise. You can begin to reclaim your personal power and free choice. Pia Mellody's description of this process can help you intervene in any addictive cycle:

Love Addiction Cycle:

1. You feel a longing for connection.
2. Your partner pulls away.
3. Your stress rises and you become obsessed with your partner.
4. You compulsively reject your partner or do anything to keep that person from leaving.
5. If your partner stays, you feel relief until the next time your partner withdraws and the cycle starts again.

Breaking The Love Addiction Cycle:

1. You feel a longing for connection.
2. Your partner pulls away.
3. Your stress rises and you become obsessed with your partner.

4. You stop, breathe, feel your emotions, keep from acting or speaking compulsively and you get support.
5. Your self-esteem rises as you take care of yourself and let the relationship take its natural course. You begin to free yourself from the cycle.

When you break the addictive cycle, you may have to "detoxify" from the person you are addicted to just as an alcoholic withdraws from alcohol. If you can focus on yourself and ask for support from people who understand what you are going through, you can deepen your recovery through this process. As you stay with yourself you can trace your deepest feelings to their source — usually the neglect and abandonment you experienced as a child.

If you were raised in a dysfunctional family system, it is necessary to heal your underlying co-dependency (your family of origin issues) as well as your addictions. Each time you choose not to act on your addiction and you go to the source of your yearning for connection, you take a step towards health. As you heal your childhood issues you will have less need to turn to addictions to cover your pain and to give you the feeling of connection you wanted as a child. As your self-love grows you may find that you care too much about yourself to put yourself through another addictive cycle.

Building A Relationship With Yourself

It is important to take care of yourself as you free yourself from addiction. To do this you need to build your physical health, concentrate on your emotional and spiritual growth, and move toward being a fully conscious person. You may find that if you work on yourself and stay open, you will naturally let go of unhealthy relationships and healthier relationships will come into your life.

As you heal from your co-dependency and addictions, you may need to experience different relationships. You may slip into old patterns and addictive behaviors along the way. This is part of the journey towards health.

Remember, as a child in a dysfunctional home you simply were not taught how to be intimate. You probably had few healthy role models. This is no reflection on you. You cannot expect to know what you are not taught. Fortunately, it is never too late to learn.

Fear Of Engulfment

As you continue to build your sense of yourself, you will probably have less fear that you will "lose" yourself in a relationship. As with many co-dependents, you may fear that if you give fully of yourself, you will not be able to be your own person.

If you feel that getting involved in a relationship would destroy you and that you are only safe in isolation, you are living with a relationship phobia. If you have developed fantasies about romantic relationships, love may seem more pure when you are alone and dreaming of a lover than when you actually live with someone day to day. But as Earnie Larsen says,

> "People may 'feel' love but the reality of love is lived out in the context of a relationship, or it remains just a feeling."
>
> *Stage II Recovery*

If you are addicted, you will tend to be more afraid of engulfment. You fear that if you let someone know you, he or she will challenge you about your addictions. Because your addictions can be such an important part of your life, you may feel if someone takes them away, that person will control your reality. Your fear is actually not that you will lose your *self* in a relationship, but that you would lose your *addictions*.

If you are relatively free of addiction and have a clear sense of yourself, you will probably not have the same fear of having your reality controlled. You will not need to hide your compulsions from your partner out of fear that they will be taken away. You will have nothing to lose.

The truth is it is impossible to lose yourself in another person. This is a co-dependent myth. You may *feel* lost because you never had the chance to gain a sure sense of yourself. You can doubt yourself and feel confused in a relationship, and you may become addicted to another person. Beneath your struggles your true self remains whole, waiting to connect with safe people. Your true self may feel afraid to come out, but it is most likely that under the fear of being engulfed you are afraid of being hurt and abandoned again.

Fear Of Abandonment

It can take time and patience to heal your fear of abandonment and to learn to trust in the present. It is important to understand that your self-esteem becomes very low when you are terrified of abandonment. If you can keep this in mind and remember how vulnerable you are because of your past, you can have compassion for yourself as you cultivate your self-love and explore intimacy with others. Because of your past experience you also can take special care to invite safe, non-toxic people into your life.

As we mentioned earlier, a toxic person is someone whose behavior and attitudes leave you feeling anxious or on guard. If you are with a non-toxic person who is self-responsible and non-abusive, your Inner Child will probably sense that it is safe to explore intimacy with that person.

Healthy Self-Protection

As you recover and reach a higher level of self-differentiation, making thoughtful choices will probably come more easily to you. You can be less controlled by your emotions. You can consider carefully what is best for you and choose someone with whom you can be yourself. This may feel awkward at first if you are used to denying your needs and adapting yourself to others. Taking care of yourself may go against all you were taught as a child. It is the only way, however, to open yourself to be fully loving with another person.

An important part of taking care of yourself is looking ahead to the future. You can begin to think about the rest of your life and what you want and need for yourself. You can make a commitment to your long-term growth and happiness. If you can plan for your emotional and spiritual future, you will be less likely to compromise yourself for a partner or for immediate gratification. This does not diminish your need to live one day at a time, in the now. Planning for your future does not need to take you out of the present but simply provide you with healthy guidance, as a responsible parent would do for a child.

The Right To Choose

Choosing healthy people to share your life with may sound simple enough. However, we have seen the ways in which you can be unconsciously lured into dysfunctional relationships. If you do not treat your co-dependency and addictions, you will probably continue to be attracted to people who are at a similar level of self-differentiation as you and with whom you can recreate the unhealthy relationships of your past. As you become more aware of your unconscious motivations you can avoid what Terence Gorski calls *selection error*. In his tape, *Addictive Relationships*, Gorski claims that relationships fail primarily because people choose partners who are not appropriate for them.

If you are from a dysfunctional family, you probably believe that you do not have the right to select a partner from different people with whom you are close. You can be so accustomed to denying your needs and preferences, it does not occur to you that you have an inherent right to make a selection. In your recovery you can reclaim your power to choose and learn to make decisions that are in your best interest.

The Freedom To Leave

Just as it is up to you to pick a healthy partner, it is your choice to remain in a relationship. As you become less prone to addiction, you may let go of the belief that you are a victim and that you are compelled to stay in an unfulfilling relationship. Healthy love requires that you maintain a sense of your personal power and freedom in your relationship. As Gorski says in his tape *Addictive Relationships*, "Love is a free expression of choice." When you know you can leave a relationship, your decision to stay comes from health not addiction.

You may need to try a number of relationships before you find someone you could live with for the rest of your life. It may happen that after an initial period of getting to know one another you find you and your partner do not have enough in common to deepen your commitment. In that case it is healthy to part as friends. This is wise and very different from running from one person to the next in order not to be alone.

If you were raised in an enmeshed family system, you probably did not learn how to separate from your parents in a loving, responsible way as you grew older. This can leave you confused about how to end relationships with people in the present. When you are not taught how to separate, you may either cut off from your partner abusively or stay in an unhealthy situation. Both of these extremes can be harmful.

It is never too late to learn to separate in a clean, loving way. If you feel it is best for you to end a relationship, you may want to take time to get your thoughts clear about what you will say to your partner. You might want to talk with friends about what you are doing and share your feelings with them.

When you tell your partner that you want to separate, it is often helpful to say what you like about your partner and what you liked about the relationship. You may acknowledge the ways in which the relationship has been a growing experience for you, if that is true. As you become more comfortable separating from people, you may find that you can maintain respect and love for your partner, even if you need to end the relationship.

Go Slowly

If you can keep from acting out of addiction, you can take care of yourself at each stage of a relationship. For instance, it is appropriate not to share everything about yourself on your first date. Healthy people test each other to see if it is safe to share in the future. Try sharing a little and then stopping to see what happens next:

- Is the other person honoring you?
- Do you feel comfortable being yourself with this person?
- What is your gut and your inner knowledge telling you?

It is also healthy to be aware of *your* behavior: Are you honoring the other person's sharing and being "present" with him or her?

Chemistry

When you learn about the unconscious attractions that can pull you into unhealthy relationships, it may be tempting to distrust an initial attraction you have for another person. You may wonder if there is such a thing as healthy attraction. As you weed out your addictions, however, you can learn to distinguish between a healthy, vital attraction and an *addictive charge*.

When you are attracted out of addiction, you usually feel desperate to be with a partner. Healthy chemistry is an easy, supportive feeling. Two people just seem to flow with each other. The relationship usually begins with a friendship and the intimacy of the friendship develops into a more sexual attraction. This can be exciting but not in an addictive way. This initial excitement can deepen into a closeness of two people sharing parts of each other's lives.

So Far So Good?

If you feel comfortable being yourself with a person and the relationship continues, it is helpful to check in with yourself now and then. If you can, try to use your discernment and see the relationship clearly every step of the way. Watch to see if your partner takes you for granted or if he or she is often inconsistent. Notice if your partner disregards your feelings. It is especially important to see whether your partner wants the same level of intimacy that you want. If not, you may need to move on to avoid selection error. You may want to affirm to yourself that you are worthy of the intimacy you want and need. It is important to trust your intuition on these matters. You can remind yourself that there is little point in trying to build trust with someone who is not supportive and trustworthy.

Taking care of yourself and noticing the progress of a relationship does not require that you are constantly tense and on guard. As you gain a stronger sense of yourself, you can flow with your partner while you stay conscious and clear about what you need.

Inter-dependency

If you can take care of yourself in a relationship you can learn to be *inter-dependent* with your partner, rather than co-dependent. This means you can be intensely connected and bonded with your partner and yet maintain your unique, precious self. You can allow yourself to be vulnerable and loving and still feel your strength and your personal power. When you are clear about who you are you can be fully yourself with another person. This is a sign of high self-differentiation and true spiritual health.

It may help to remind yourself that developing this level of health is a process. It does not happen all at once. You probably will not become fully independent and then deeply bond with someone. You can go back and forth between taking care of yourself and your relationship. You may think to yourself, "I'm starting to lose my focus, my clear sense of myself. Maybe I need to be alone or to have dinner with a friend tonight." You let your partner know what you decide to do so you do not behave addictively and cut off from your partner. In this way, you can take care of yourself and still be loving and gentle with your partner. This is what intimacy is all about. It is about flowing between closeness and living the rest of your life without breaking the spiritual connection with your partner.

"I'm Something Without You"

To get a sense of the degree to which you are interdependent with your partner ask yourself, "What would happen to me if my partner left or died?" Do you feel that you would be able to grieve the loss and still live a meaningful life without that person?

It is healthy to sense the tremendous loss you would feel if you were no longer with the one you love, and how much you would miss your partner's special qualities. In fact, no one could ever replace that unique person. If you lose a significant person, you will feel deep grief and you may think that you will never find another person similar to your partner. This is true. You can never replace a person in your life. Through the grieving process, however, you can let go, move on and eventually be open to new relationships. A key to this process is knowing that your feelings of loss are not a permanent state of being. It is unhealthy to believe that without your partner you would have nothing — no matter how noble this may sound.

You would hope that the one you love cares about you in a healthy way. If your partner tells you how much he or she loves you and how much the relationship has added to the beauty of his or her life, that is healthy. If your partner says how painfully hard it would be without you but that he or she would be able to survive, you are doing well. But, if your partner believes that he or she could not live without you and that you are the only thing that makes life worth living, you and your partner may need to seek help. You are probably dealing with co-dependency and addiction, not love and intimacy.

Outside Interference

Although it is important to keep from becoming en-meshed with your partner by maintaining your sense of yourself and having your own friends and interests, it is also healthy to protect the relationship from being invaded by outside forces.

As Sharon Wegscheider-Cruse explains, in her book *Coupleship*, *invaders* are people, behaviors and substances that can undermine your relationship. This does not mean that you need to be afraid that everyone's demands for your attention will destroy your relationship. But you should try to set reasonable limits on the time and atten-tion demanded of you from outside the relationship. It is important to put your relationship first.

How can you do this practically? Look back over a few weeks or months. Ask yourself how much time you have given to your primary relationship and how much time to other people and activities: to friends, parents, children, alcohol, drugs, nicotine, food, TV, sports, gambling and work. Ask yourself how often you give your relationship priority. If you have to choose between doing something with your partner or with a friend, whom do you choose and how often? If your partner never or rarely comes first, you may need better boundaries between your rela-tionship and the outside world.

Balance

Ashley started to see me when she realized that she felt no intimacy with her husband. For the last ten years she had been playing golf two or three times a week, taking tennis lessons and otherwise building more of a relation-ship with her sports activities than with her husband. She woke up one day and realized she had no one she could talk to on a gut level. She felt jealous of her husband who had a number of close friends. Over the years he had asked Ashley to give more time to their marriage but she had not responded to his needs. He began to put his free time into developing his relationships and now he was living with the results: healthy, intimate friendships rather than activities.

As Ashley worked through her feelings in therapy, she was able to get in touch with her true self and her needs for love and attention. She chose to cut down on her sports activities and began to put more energy into her relationship with her husband. She also began to cultivate her friendships. Intimacy in her life became her focus and sports changed from an addiction to a preference. It took her a couple of years to ease up on her compulsive behavior but she eventually found a balance between her marriage, her friendships and her activities.

Triangles: In-Laws And Children

It may be challenging for you and your partner to keep your relationship from being invaded by other people. This is usually most difficult when it involves members of your family who interfere in your relationship.

Adam was caught in a triangle with his wife and his father. His father played the rescuer role by caring for Adam when he got drunk and by helping him financially. Adam's wife was on the outside. She was considered the "bitch" because she was always upset by Adam's irresponsibility and his father's interference in their lives. Adam accused her of not understanding him and of not being a caring wife.

When Adam finally found recovery in AA he began to think for himself and become responsible. He no longer put his wife on the outside. His father lost control over him and became so hostile, he rejected Adam for years.

Joyce's experience is another example of rigid triangles that can damage a relationship. Joyce was a young mother, married to an alcoholic. She told me, "I'll never forget how my husband would play the 'rescuer' game with the children. For example, if the kids wanted to get out of their responsibilities — go out somewhere when they were supposed to do their homework or watch TV instead of doing their chores — and I said no, Dan would come to the children's rescue and say I was being too hard on them. He would listen to what the children wanted and put on a show of reasoning with me to get me to change my mind. As this continued over the years I lost my confidence in my parenting abilities and eventually gave in to the children's demands. What undermined me the most was that Dan would say in front of the children that I was either being unreasonable or too emotional. I ended up looking like the crazy mother and he came off as the rational fair father."

The most painful part of this for Joyce, besides her gut feeling that this pattern was ineffective parenting and hurtful to the children, was she had watched her mother go through the same thing. Her father had often taken Joyce aside and told her that her mother was unfair and too strict. This made her father look like the "good guy."

Joyce often wondered how she had let herself fall into the same pattern as her mother. Because she was afraid of her husband's anger, which could easily erupt, she took care of him by avoiding any demands or confrontations that might upset him. She had been conditioned to placate. So it is not surprising that she backed down when she was blamed.

Sex Roles

Your relationship can also be invaded by subtle influences from your past. For instance, it is common to unconsciously act out the expectations relating to sex roles that you learned in your family of origin. When you are in the early stages of a relationship, it is important for you and your partner to do what you can to keep from falling into constricting sex roles.

Allison was a young mother who was also pursuing a career. Although Allison had always assumed that she would have an equal relationship with her husband, to her surprise she found that she took on her family's conception of how a woman should behave. After her wedding, she found herself running the household as she had seen all the women in her life do. She soon began to feel trapped in her marriage and resentful that she carried more of the household burden than her husband.

These gender expectations can affect men as well. The traditional male image is a significant obstacle to intimacy for men and can keep them locked in unsatisfying roles.

If you are aware of these expectations, you can work with your partner early in your relationship to keep from being limited by sex roles. This can help relieve some of the stress that you naturally feel in the early days of your marriage. Although it will most likely occur to some degree, the more you have healed your individual issues from your family of origin, the more you can keep your marriage from being sexist.

Communication

> "Words are the wings of love. If we don't verbalize what we think and feel, neither the other nor ourselves can come to a deeper understanding, a closer sharing."
>
> *Earnie Larsen and Carol Larsen Hegarty*
> *Days of Healing Days of Joy*

If you can learn to communicate openly with your partner, you will have a better chance of being fully present in your relationship while preserving a clear sense of yourself. It is especially important to be able to share your fundamental fears, wounds and needs with your partner.

Sharing honestly with another person can feel scary if you have spent years hiding your true self. You may still adhere to the "don't talk" rule of your family of origin. You may continue to believe that by repressing your feelings and thoughts, you are protecting your partner as you protected your parents. You may find that the opposite is true in a healthy relationship — if you do not share your thoughts and feelings with your partner, you can harm a relationship. When you do not share openly, you are not being fully honest. This can damage trust and create distance between you.

You may also resist communicating because you are afraid if you share who you really are, your partner will reject you. It may help to remind yourself that your partner may not be the right person for you if he or she cannot accept your true self.

Sharing can help you deepen your self-awareness. As you share your true feelings and needs, you can bring the secret unconscious parts of yourself to the surface. As long as these parts remain buried they will continue to interfere with your life. If you communicate openly with a safe partner, you make further progress on your journey toward consciousness and self-understanding. As you become more self-aware, you will be more available for intimacy.

When you share with your partner, you reflect how you experience him or her. As Gorski explains, you help to make your partner *psychologically visible*. To do this Gorski suggests you,

> "Tell them how you see them. Tell them what you think about them. Tell them what they mean to you. Tell them how you feel about them. Without that, relationships wither and die."
>
> *Addictive Relationships*

As you communicate with your partner you help make your shared experiences visible. To do this, Gorski recommends that you do things with your partner and share time together, then talk with each other about the experience. When you share, you can tell your partner:

1. "When we did (state a specific activity).
2. It meant (describe its significance to you).
3. And I felt (state your feelings) about it."

This builds shared life experiences with your partner and deepens the connection between you.

Although it is healthy to share honestly with your partner, it is important to learn to share appropriately. If you are co-dependent, you may tend towards black and white thinking and believe that you must tell your partner every detail, every specific problem and every embarrassment from your past. To do so may not be helpful and could create unnecessary tension in your relationship. On sensitive issues you may find it healthier for your relationship to share the kind of problems and issues you faced in the past without giving vivid details.

Because of the importance of communicating honestly, you want to be sure that your partner is willing to share as openly as you. If he or she is not willing to communicate openly, you may want to seek help or end the relationship if necessary.

Needs

If you are co-dependent, sharing your needs with your partner can be challenging. As you become more comfortable sharing, you can face the additional challenge of identifying your needs and believing that you have a right to have them met.

As we have seen, when you grow up in a dysfunctional home, your needs are not met on a consistent basis. This can condition you to believe that people will disregard you and reject your needs. Your fear of rejection can lead you to deny that you have needs. If you begin to acknowledge your needs, you may feel ashamed to have them. You may believe that communicating your needs would overwhelm people and scare them away. Your needs may seem desperate and secret because you had to bury them for so long. You may wonder if your needs are normal and how much is appropriate to ask of someone.

When you cannot see or admit your deepest needs, you keep yourself from getting what you truly want in life. You stay cut off from your true self. To begin to acknowledge your needs can be scary, however, because you may stir up repressed feelings from your infancy and childhood. As you get in touch with your needs you may begin to see that they were not met when you were a child. Although this can be painful, this process can help you to further let go of the fantasy bond and grieve for the neglect of your childhood. You may find that the deeper you go in your recovery, the more you will be aware of your needs, particularly your need for intimacy.

In any relationship needs will conflict and you and your partner will be unable to meet all of each other's needs. But if you are willing to express your basic needs, you may find that your partner can fulfill many of them. Asking your partner to give more than a person is capable of giving, however, only keeps you in a victim role — you can continue to assume your needs will never be met and blame your partner for failing. This can be just another defense against taking the risk to share your needs responsibly.

Communication Model

It is especially important in an intimate relationship for you to be able to tell your partner how you feel when he or she acts in ways that upset you. If you share your feelings and needs gently and clearly, you can stay vulnerable with your partner. This makes it easier for your partner to stay vulnerable and you will probably have a better chance of resolving problems between you. If you and your partner can learn to share your needs and resolve disagreements in a loving way, you can keep your relationship honest and clear. You can avoid much misunderstanding and keep the relationship from being clouded by unresolved issues and resentments.

Remember that it takes time to become comfortable sharing your feelings about your partner's behavior. It is helpful to be patient with yourself and know that you will probably not express yourself perfectly. You may worry about your partner's reaction. You may feel afraid of rejection and want to run away or reject your partner. If you can let your feelings flow through you and stay clear with your needs, you can grow through these experiences.

To become more comfortable sharing your needs, you can use a communications model similar to the one we looked at for sharing life experiences. When you have feelings about something that your partner does, try telling him or her:

1. I feel (state your feeling) when you (state the specific behavior).
2. I need (state a specific need).

Do your best to stay with "I" statements and to avoid blaming the other person. This helps you to stay clear with your issues and to keep from attacking your partner.

After you have shared, notice what your partner does. If he or she is willing to accommodate on a reasonable issue, watch if the behavior changes in the way that you need. If your partner respects your need or is willing to negotiate, then you will know you were heard. As we will see, there will be times when your partner needs to say no to your need. However, if he or she often refuses to honor your needs, this could be a warning sign for you. Trust your intuition and note if your partner's resistance becomes a pattern. If so, you may not want to pursue intimacy with that person. Remember, you are worth being with someone who will listen to your needs and meet them when he or she can.

Your Needs Can Be Met

It is a wonderful experience to express a need or a particular like or dislike and have another person respond to you in a healthy way. Most co-dependents are not accustomed to this because of their past experience.

Patrick risked expressing his needs in a relationship and found positive results. Patrick had always been the pursuer in his relationships. He usually took the initiative to get together with friends and to ask women out on dates. When his friendship with Michelle developed into a romantic relationship, this pattern of his being the pursuer continued. Patrick shared with Michelle that he needed and wanted her to pursue him as well. He asked her to send him cards occasionally, leave him a love message on his answering machine, ask for special time together and plan some of their activities.

Michelle responded by regarding Patrick's need. She was healthy enough to see that Patrick was not trying to control her and that she did not have to react to him as she had to her parents. Michelle had not often pursued people in her relationships, people had usually sought her out. Therefore, this was new for her. She saw Patrick's request as a challenge for her to grow more, as well as an opportunity to honor Patrick.

No-Win Situation

When you take the risk to share your needs, you may find that your partner is unwilling to listen and negotiate with you. Although this can be a painful experience, it can help you see whether your partner is someone with whom you want to build a close relationship.

Linda learned to express her needs only to find that her partner, Charles, was not receptive to hearing them. Charles often worked overtime on his job. Linda shared with Charles that she felt sad about their situation and needed more time with him. She said she really missed him and wondered what they could work out so that they could spend more time together. Charles' response was a typically co-dependent defense. He bypassed her need and attacked Linda. Charles accused Linda of trying to control him, of being selfish and of not being understanding. When Linda reacted with shock and hurt, Charles escalated his attack. He told her that maybe things could not work out between them because she was too demanding.

This was a no-win situation. At this point Linda was talking to Charles' disease. The healthiest step for her to take was to suggest that they seek help or simply back away from the relationship and not hold on to the hope that Charles would change.

"No"

Sharing with a partner who is emotionally unavailable to you or rejects you when you express a need is quite different from negotiating with people who set appropriate limits for themselves. In a healthy relationship there will be give and take between you and your partner. You can ask your partner to meet many of your needs, and you may want to have other needs met by other significant people in your life. This is a sign of health and balance in a relationship.

In fact, you can learn to rejoice at hearing no from your partner. You can take it as a sign of health that your partner is being honest, that he or she is acting out of responsible self-care. If your partner tells you his or her limitations, your partner probably will not fall into a pattern of constantly putting your needs first. In this way you know better where you stand. There is less chance that your partner will build resentments and act out towards you in indirect ways.

Learning to rejoice when you hear no can help you set boundaries for yourself. Helping others is an essential part of living fully and expressing your love. However, just as children can help their parents in age-appropriate ways, it is important to learn to set appropriate limits on how much you are willing to do for another person as an adult.

It is loving to be helpful and to occasionally go beyond your limits for your partner. However, if you continually act out of a rigid pattern of behavior and at the expense of yourself, often in the face of promises that your spouse will change, you are trapped in an unhealthy situation.

When your partner expresses a need, you may want to consider the request and ask yourself if it is something you are willing to do. Does it feel clear inside of you? Listen to your initial gut reaction. You may want to be mindful when you do something that your partner could easily do. It is a sign of caring to be responsible *to* another person — to be able to respond appropriately. You can slip into unhealthy behavior, however, when you try to be responsible *for* other people and do what they need to do for themselves.

Although it is up to you to find your limits, I believe that each of us must learn to be physically and financially independent in a healthy way. If you are not willing to take care of yourself, regardless of the situation, you will most likely end up unhappy and unsatisfied. I do not mean to suggest that you must do everything alone. You can have support, encouragement and close sharing with others and still be able to stand on your own when necessary. This flexibility is a sign of wholeness and high self-differentiation, which frees you to love with an open heart.

Needless

If you continue to deny your needs as an adult and do not share them with people in your life, you may become *needless* as a defense. You may try to control how much you allow yourself to feel and what needs you choose to have met. You may try to appear tough and expect others to be the same. Under the surface, however, you can be extremely vulnerable because you have stifled your true needs for so long. The irony is that as you continue to deny your needs, they will only increase unconsciously.

It is likely you will do anything to avoid feeling your needs. When you do not express your needs directly, you will invariably act them out "sideways." For instance, if your needs are triggered, you may distance yourself from your partner to protect yourself from acknowledging your needs. Many couples will keep their deep need for connection and closeness suppressed. When they do, they are not able to sustain intimacy for any significant period of time.

Tom And Karen

Tom and Karen were a young couple who had been together for several months. They both grew up in dysfunctional homes and had not been given enough nurturing as infants. Their parents, who were alcoholic, had been unable to be fully present with their children. They did not hold their children nor meet their needs regularly in the way that children need.

Often when Tom and Karen were emotionally open to one another and would deepen their vulnerability by being sexual, they experienced a backlash. These took different forms at different times. Sometimes Tom became very quiet and withdrawn after their intimacy. Karen would feel abandoned and react with anger. Tom would then accuse Karen of trying to control and trap him and would push her farther away. Neither partner acknowledged that their intimacy had tapped into their tremendous needs for closeness and had touched off deep abandonment fears in both of them.

For Tom, being vulnerable touched off his unconscious need for his mother and his anger that she had not been emotionally available to him as a child. But instead of feeling his need for closeness and his fear of abandonment, Tom turned to a familiar defense: He protected himself from his unconscious feelings by emotionally pulling away from Karen.

In response, Karen would not let Tom know how much it hurt her when he pulled away so suddenly. She denied her vulnerability and the wounds from her childhood. Instead she would get angry at Tom over a triviality. This would lead to a fight that was not about the real issues between them. After they fought and had enough distance to feel "composed" again, they would come back together and try again.

Sarah And Bruce

Sarah and Bruce also turned to defensive behaviors to avoid their deepest issues. After a short period of emotional and sexual closeness, Sarah would shut down. She could not understand why she did this and she did not talk about it with Bruce. She would just become very busy and preoccupied. Bruce would feel abandoned and hurt, but feel too ashamed of his emotions to share them with Sarah. He would retaliate in the ways he had learned in his unhealthy family of origin by criticizing Sarah's activities or friends.

Both of these couples related on the level of defenses, oblivious to the real issues beneath the surface — their deep need for intimacy, their fear of abandonment and their pain from their dysfunctional childhoods. They had been raised to assume that being vulnerable always led to getting hurt. Both couples sought help for their problems. They gradually learned to distinguish between problems in the present and the deeper issues from their pasts. This helped them to support each other in recovery instead of undermining each other.

Responsibility

For you and your partner to support each other, you both can learn to risk sharing your deepest needs and your most vulnerable feelings. As you grow in recovery you will be better able to distinguish between feelings that originate from your childhood and present-day feelings. This can help you avoid projecting the issues from your childhood onto your partner. When you project your fears onto your partner, you do not see your partner as he or she really is. You see a displaced image of your parents. This can be an unconscious defense mechanism that keeps you from connecting your deepest feelings to your relationship with your parents.

As you learn not to project your issues onto your partner, you become more responsible in your relationship. Instead of pushing your partner away because of your unconscious fears, you choose to share your memories and feelings with your partner. You can invite your partner to journey with you and support you as you heal from your past. You may find that this will further your recovery and make the healing process safer and gentler.

If you and your partner are both co-dependent, you probably will not be able to reach this level of vulnerability unless you both are in recovery. Therapy and 12-Step support groups can help you become more conscious of the issues from your pasts and be responsible with how you handle these issues today. With support you can choose not to play games with one another. You can risk sharing your true selves. If you and your partner can go to this deeper level of vulnerability, your relationship can be grounded in reality and you will open yourselves to intimacy.

Control

As you learn to share your needs responsibly, at times you may feel a strong urge to try to control how your partner responds to you. In the first chapter, we saw that an urge to control is a primary symptom of co-dependency. If you were raised in a dysfunctional family system you may have believed that if you did not control your parents and your siblings, the family would fall apart. You probably did not see conflicts resolved in healthy ways. In most dysfunctional family systems, when people disagree, they turn to manipulation and abuse to try to control others, instead of resolving issues fairly.

One client who struggled with the issue of control told me, "I was in control of everybody in my life and not feeling any feelings. I didn't know there was any other way to be until I began recovery for my co-dependency. I knew what I was supposed to do and I knew what everyone else was supposed to do. If someone disagreed with me, I made sure they saw it my way. Now I'm confused but I understand that is good for me and that it's a stage I need to go through in recovery."

To begin to let go of your urge to control you may want to remind yourself that you simply cannot make another person into something he or she is not. You can say how you feel in reaction to other people's behavior, but you have no power to change that behavior.

You may fall into a common co-dependent trap of believing that a change in your behavior can solve the problems between you and your partner. You may tell yourself, "This time it will be different. I will be more thoughtful and understanding. If I change, we will be able to get along fine." This can be a way to avoid grieving because you and your partner are simply not compatible.

Sometimes even if your partner is in recovery, his or her basic nature may not be right for you. You do not need to criticize your partner because he or she is different. It is healthiest for you to accept that you cannot change the person and that you need to take care of yourself.

Unless a person's behavior is abusive to you or something you cannot tolerate, you can try to appreciate different ways of doing things. You could see this experience as a challenge to accept your personality differences and see how your partner's unique perceptions add to the richness of your life.

The truth is most things are beyond your control and control over another person is an illusion. Just as you could not control your troubled parents, you cannot control your partner. It is healthier to replace our concept of "power over" someone with that of personal power — being in charge of your own choices.

As you recover you will become clearer about when you can assert your personal power and when it is beneficial to let a process unfold. You will become more flexible. You will flow with life naturally.

Your Relationship Has A Higher Power

Although it goes against all that you were taught as a child, in any relationship you can only do your part, maintain your integrity and allow other people to make their own choices. It is a paradox but if you take care of yourself and let the relationship take its natural course, you will have a better chance of finding a fulfilling relationship.

It is important to remember that the future of the relationship is in the hands of your Higher Power, the Spirit of the Universe. You cannot know for certain if a relationship is the right one. You cannot force intimacy or follow certain steps to ensure a successful relationship.

There are no guarantees. A relationship needs to unfold in its own way. Each relationship is a learning experience for you. If a relationship does not turn out the way you had hoped, you can look at your part in why it ended, but it is usually not helpful to find fault with yourself because the relationship did not work out. It is most healing to see each relationship as part of a larger journey and to try to be gentle with yourself along the way.

Flowing Intimacy

As you and your partner learn to honor each other's needs, negotiate with open hearts and let go of control, you can maintain the flow of your relationship through your disagreements.

If there is no major decision hanging on a difference of opinion, you can practice making the transition from a disagreement to the continuation of your normal activities. Assume that you and your partner are involved in a heated discussion that is going nowhere. You may want to try taking a deep breath and saying, "We can continue this later. Let's get together at three o'clock to talk more. Now let's do our errands or go out and do whatever we need to."

Before you end your discussion you can reassure your partner that you still love him or her. You may even want to tell your partner that you will not abandon his or her Inner Child. You can commit to each other that you will get together at a later time and eventually resolve the issue. Sometimes it takes a few breaks in a discussion for each person to process what is going on with him or her.

If you can make a smooth transition, you can build faith in your relationship. You can see that a disagreement does not need to destroy your love for each other. As you do this you will feel stronger inside. Your Inner Child will be happy that you did not abandon him or her and you will have all the energy that you might otherwise have let drain out if you had not taken care of yourself.

The Cycle Of A Healthy Relationship

As Gorski explains on his audiocassette, when you can work through disagreements in a loving way, you can create a cycle of deepening contentment. This cycle replaces the addictive patterns of rejecting one another or becoming further enmeshed when there is conflict in the relationship. Gorski describes this cycle in the following way:

1. You and your partner feel satisfaction and contentment with each other.
2. A problem develops that creates pain.
3. You and your partner turn to problem-solving behavior. You rationally look at the problem and work together to solve it. You seek outside help if necessary.
4. When the problem is solved, intimacy is heightened. You return to the normal state of being content and satisfied with each other.

Addictive Relationships
Why Love Goes Wrong In Recovery

There is little struggle in this healthy cycle. It is flowing, safe and consistent. You can be yourself without fearing excessive reactions from your partner. You can count on your partner and know what to expect from him or her. The relationship flows most of the time. You and your partner experience occasional problems and work them through together. As you solve your problems you can treat each other with respect, caring and patience. There is no need for any form of abuse.

If you had unhealthy role models in your life, you may believe that all relationships are a struggle. However, because they are consistent and flowing, healthy relationships are much easier than addictive ones. If you have lived through addictive relationships, a healthy relationship may seem almost effortless by comparison. It may feel a little awkward to adjust to a smooth relationship if you are used to an addictive cycle, but you will probably learn to enjoy it in time.

Adjusting to a healthy relationship can mean letting go of a lifetime of living through the pain of enmeshment and addictive cycles. You may have become accustomed to holding on to the few good moments that are occasional calms in a stormy relationship. You may still believe, on some level, that swinging from ecstasy to despair and back again is a sign of true love.

The truth is healthy intimacy cannot flourish in such relationships. To fully give your heart to another person, you need to know where you stand on a consistent basis. You need to be able to build a certainty about how your partner will behave in different situations.

If you and your partner can have fair, clean discussions and are willing to work together long enough to resolve conflicts, you will have a better chance to maintain intimacy. You will be comfortable knowing that your basic needs will be met and happy knowing you can have many of your wants. You will be able to have all of this if your relationship is based on nurturing and conflict-resolution. These are the most important elements in a relationship. With these to build upon, there will be fertile ground for the other characteristics of a healthy relationship to grow: communication, respect, honesty, the sharing of feelings, intimacy, commitment, fun and trust.

Being vulnerable opens you to the true miracle of love — that you can have conflicts, be less than perfect, see that your partner is not perfect, hurt and suffer for those imperfections and feel anger, and yet love is always reborn. Each time your love for your partner is reborn it grows stronger, because it is based less on illusions, expectations and hope for a fantasy bond. It grows out of really knowing another person, really being intimate with the many sides of your partner and yourself.

Caring And Closeness

As you learn to take care of *yourself* in a relationship, and you and your partner take care of the *relationship*, you can finally experience the caring and closeness for which you may have yearned for so long.

In recovery you can free yourself from your longing for parental love and gradually heal the inner emptiness that leads you into addictions. You can begin to explore healthy ways of loving with a safe partner of your choice.

You learn that love begins within yourself and is a gift that you can share with others. You begin to gain a sense of personal power as you take care of your Inner Child, rather than demanding or expecting someone take care of you. You find that you can love and care for another self-respecting individual in healthy, appropriate ways. You and your partner can work to meet each other's needs as best you can. You no longer need strive to romance someone else's Inner Child, promising in a fever of love and courtship to take care of that person at the expense of your own spirit.

You will have the courage to live fully and to share your aliveness with a special person who is compatible with you in recovery and in a zest for life. It will be a relationship in which you can be responsible *to* another (caring), but not responsible *for* the person (control). You can have a love that is based on solid friendship and honesty.

You will experience a closeness, a happiness, a delicious sense of how beautiful your own and another person's spirits can be. You can feel a relaxed enjoyment of shared companionship and fun. You can learn to flow between a deep sense of oneness and bonding with your partner and your sense of yourself as a unique, precious person.

Some Things To Do:
Honoring Your Needs And Wants

Again, find a safe quiet place. Open yourself to the universe and to your Inner Child. Listen to that gentle voice from deep inside of you.

Using the hand you usually do not write with, write what you would have liked from your parents as a child.

Let yourself go and honor whatever comes to you. Allow yourself to have all of your wishes and needs. You are worth the smallest gesture (a wave goodbye after your father dropped you off at school) and the biggest commitment (taking time every night to sit and talk, to listen to you, to read stories, whatever you would like).

If feelings come up, such as anger and sadness, really let yourself feel them. What you did not get as a child can never be replaced. You need to mourn that. It may feel painful to acknowledge this but it is the only way to heal from your past.

Starting today you can make sure that your Inner Child gets as many of his or her needs met as possible. You may want to look over what you wrote and see how many of those things you can have today. You may be able to give them to yourself, and you may have friends who can give you what you want if you ask.

You are worth being honored and nurtured. Your needs were precious as a child and they are still precious today. As you acknowledge your needs you will be more open to meet the needs of others in healthy ways. You may find, to your surprise, that there is plenty to go around. Unlike your family of origin, you and those close to you can meet each others' needs and feel fulfilled.

5

Never Too Late

There comes a time when you realize that your parents are going to get old someday. Perhaps they have already aged and settled into retirement. You may have thought about what will happen to them. Do you wonder about their finances, about nursing homes and about coping with their deaths? These are common concerns. It is a natural part of the life cycle for parents to become more dependent on their children when they grow older. Healthy families adjust to these changes. The children are able to feel respect and affection for their parents and help them without neglecting themselves.

If you grew up in a family where emotions were repressed and tensions unresolved, you may struggle with how to care for your aging parents. You may be in the process of healing from the neglect and abuse of your childhood. Your feelings of anger and sadness about your past may be so strong that you do not feel capable of helping your parents as they grow older.

The effects of co-dependency and addictions on your parents can be cumulative, resulting in physical, emotional and financial problems. The more enmeshed you are with your parents, the more difficult it can be to remain balanced in relation to them at this time. Your parents may become more isolated as they grow older. The few friends they have had during their lives may move away or die. Your parents may not be good at making new friends because of their problems with intimacy, their lack of confidence or their failing health. They can become lonely and needy. Your parents may look to you for companionship, to give their lives more meaning. This change in their lives can be particularly difficult for you if they have always been very active and social.

If you are co-dependent, you may react in familiar ways to the problems of your aging parents — you may fall into self-destructive caretaking behaviors. When you see your parents becoming weaker and more dependent, you may try to do more for them than is appropriate. As you did as a child, you may abandon yourself for them. If you do, you may become resentful and frustrated and act abusively towards your parents without meaning to. You may even have an unconscious urge to punish them for all the years that you took care of them. Acting on this would probably hurt you in the long run and it certainly would be harmful to your parents.

If you can avoid punishing your parents for the past and change your behavior towards them in the present, you may face different challenges. When you try to help your parents in appropriate ways and maintain your personal boundaries, you may be accused of not doing enough. They may still expect you to show your love by putting their needs before yours. When you do not behave as they expect, they may become controlling, resistant and uncooperative.

Sometimes parents change in ways you do not anticipate. I have seen parents who had been overprotective and controlling begin to let go as they get older. They become less concerned with themselves and start thinking about whether you will be all right when they are gone. This can be just as challenging for you as when they remain set in their ways.

Joe's father had been distant and unsupportive most of Joe's life. As Joe's father aged, something changed inside of him. He began to be more emotionally available to Joe. He was able to talk with his son about the past and about his life in the present. When his father was willing to open up to him, Joe felt a strong urge to show his love. This was not a burden but an open, loving feeling that came alive inside of Joe. Joe wanted with all his heart to buy his father a Cadillac. His father had always wanted a Cadillac but had never got one for himself. Joe began to save money and he and his father planned a trip together in the new car.

As Joe's father changed he became very loving to Joe's five-year-old son. Although Joe could not relive his childhood, this affection for his son helped to make up for the intimacy that Joe had not received from his father.

Joe's father died just after he and Joe had grown closer. This was devastating for Joe. He felt abandoned again by his father. He told me in a therapy session, "My father could have lived if he wanted to. Why didn't he want to live? Everything was finally coming together. Why didn't he want to be with me? Why did he leave me?"

It took time for Joe to grieve the loss of his father. Often events in his life would trigger his feelings for his father. For instance, his abandonment feelings would come out if I made plans to travel. His Inner Child would become very sad. He learned to focus most of these feelings on his father, where they originated.

I encouraged Joe to connect with his father spiritually and to talk quietly with him. When Joe resisted opening up to his father because of the painful memories from earlier in his life, I reminded Joe that his father's true spirit would never harm him. This made it safe for Joe to carry his father's spirit with him. He was able to feel the love they had shared and sense his father's support, even though he had died. As he did this, Joe felt even closer to his father and could appreciate all the positive memories he had of him.

As Joe's experience shows, it is possible to recapture your lost love for a parent, even if the parent has passed away.

If your parents are still alive it is not always possible to predict how they will react as you change your behavior towards them. Whether or not your parents change, if you are an adult with aging parents, you have a wonderful opportunity to learn about empathy and its healthy expression. You can explore the limits of what you can and cannot do for another person. You may find that as you continue to grow, you can feel empathy for your parents, even if they are still unable to give you the unconditional love and approval you always wanted. As you heal your Inner Child who is so needy for parents' love, you will find it easier to reach out to your parents in the present.

In spite of the struggles with their families, most co-dependents, deep in their hearts, do not want to abandon their parents. In recovery, you can learn to take care of yourself, maintain your personal boundaries and still give to your aging parents in appropriate, loving ways.

When You Really Care, You Hurt

Taking care of your parents in co-dependent ways does not truly help them and is damaging to you. If you are just beginning to learn about co-dependency, this may not be clear to you.

Lois told me, "I was always concerned with not upsetting my parents. All of my life I thought of their needs and how I could comfort them and make their lives easier. When they retired, they seemed worn out by their emotional traumas. They seemed to need even more help. I felt they had suffered enough and could not be expected to cope with anything more.

"My parents' health deteriorated when they retired. My mother had arthritis that she refused to treat in a sensible way. Her knee joints hurt her very much but she would not watch her weight or her salt intake. She would not exercise and she would not do anything to relieve her emotional tension. Instead she went to doctors who experimented on her with drugs that made her sick, gave her high blood pressure and affected her mentally.

"Every week, it seemed, concerned friends suggested ways to help my mother. They knew people whose arthritis had been alleviated by a change in diet, by exercise programs or by other kinds of treatment. My mother resisted any suggestions to seek further help. She seemed committed to the idea that her condition was hopeless and that she deserved admiration for the way she endured her pain.

"I knew that different treatments might not cure her arthritis but I believed they could ease her suffering. I felt very angry towards her when I realized she had acted this way all of my life. She had always imposed unnecessary limitations on herself. As far as I could tell she believed her sole purpose in life was to 'make the best of a bad situation.'

"I wanted to tell my mother that she could choose not to suffer, but I couldn't bring myself to confront her. I felt I would be betraying her at the end of her life. I kept thinking, 'She's suffered enough. If I'm honest with her, she'll think I've turned against her.'

"I was overwhelmed because I felt I had submerged my feelings in hers. I had a sense that I could feel my mother's fear of improving her life. She would not allow herself to reach out, to risk new things and strive to be healthy. Her family had taught her that a person could not grow and change. She was more afraid of breaking the family rules than of living another 20 years in pain.

"I knew that I was also caught in family rules. By not telling her how I felt, I was doing what our family had always done and was going along with her decision to suffer and jeopardize her life. I was so confused. I couldn't sort out my thoughts and feelings. As far as I could tell, any choice I made would be the wrong one."

You may experience similar feelings as your parents grow older. Lois' struggle is a familiar one for co-dependents. The ways you learned to take care of your parents, who seemed unable to cope with life when you were a child, can run very deep within you. When your parents actually do become more dependent and less able to function because of their age, the co-dependent feelings from your childhood can resurface. You may find yourself wanting to rescue them as you tried to do for so many years. As you heal from your past it will be easier to distinguish healthy concern for your parents from familiar urges to caretake. You will also find that you will have less difficulty making thoughtful decisions and taking appropriate action.

A Typical Crisis

Often, a crisis can force you to become involved with your aging parents whether you feel ready or not. If you can take care of yourself through such incidents, you may find them to be valuable opportunities for you to grow. I have heard many variations of the following story involving retired parents.

Lena's parents were a retired couple who let their financial affairs slip into disarray. Lena's father had always taken care of financial matters and her mother had managed to make ends meet. The reduction in income since their retirement had overwhelmed them but they had not addressed their problems. Lena's father refused to face the situation and her mother seemed to have just given up.

Lena regularly received letters from her parents in which they only hinted at their problems. It was not until she visited them at Christmas that she realized how bad things were. She discovered that if their affairs were not straightened out quickly, they would lose their house and be impoverished.

Lena had a sister, Jenny, who was a compulsive spender. Jenny had developed a problem with money as a child, and had always been the needy fragile child. Her parents had always gone out of their way to help her. To get attention from her parents Jenny learned to be weak, immature and irresponsible. She often got into trouble and constantly spent her parents' money. Jenny's parents contributed to her problems by continuing to support her financially. They believed they showed their love for their daughter by giving her more money. On an unconscious level Jenny also served as a distraction for her parents. As long as they focused their attention on Jenny, they could avoid looking at their own problems.

In the family system, since Jenny was the child who was unable to cope, Lena was expected to be strong and take care of herself. Her parents often told Lena that she could handle her problems on her own. This left Lena confused and hurt — her parents complimented her for her strength but subtly abandoned her because of it. Because of her role in the family, Lena learned to be financially independent at an early age. As she grew older she would have liked to borrow money from her parents for a new car or a down-payment on a condominium, but she knew her parents would refuse.

While Lena learned to support herself, her parents spent money on Jenny, who was usually in debt. They continued to help her out of financial trouble, even after she was married. Her husband, Allen, had similar problems with money. Several times Lena's parents came to her to borrow money to pay off the rising debts of Jenny and Allen.

On her Christmas visit Lena discovered that Jenny and Allen had mismanaged a real estate venture and had borrowed almost $50,000 from the family which they were unable to pay back. This pushed Lena's parents deeper into financial crisis. When Lena confronted her parents about this matter, she found that the dysfunctional patterns of her childhood were still intact. Although Jenny had left home and married, her parents still felt she was too fragile to take care of herself. They told Lena that she was insensitive to Jenny and hinted that Lena should bail out her sister.

In addition to the drain on their income from Jenny and her husband, Lena's parents had developed drug habits. Lena's father took Valium daily to reduce his anxiety and control his high blood pressure. He also misused pain medication that had been prescribed for his arthritis. He had become addicted and was unwilling to look at his problem. Lena's mother was frightened by his condition but was afraid to take him off the medication. She worried that without the drugs, he would be tense and difficult to live with, that his blood pressure would rise and he might have a heart attack. She rationalized his drug abuse by saying that at his age he should not have to suffer.

Lena's mother also misused drugs, making her less willing to look at her husband's problem. She took pain killers for a back problem. The drugs gave her severe diarrhea that weakened her. The drugs made her groggy much of the time, to the point that she was afraid to drive a car. She refused to talk with her physician about these side effects and the worse she felt, the more he increased her dosage.

On her visit Lena found herself overwhelmed by her parents' problems. She felt powerless and confused. She wanted to help but she shuddered to think of once again pouring all her energy and money into her family, and felt angry, knowing her family would never appreciate her efforts, even if she put her life on hold to help them. She wondered how to show her love for her parents without abandoning herself.

"I *Am* Loving!"

Lena's experiences in recovery from co-dependency gave her the guidance she needed to follow her intuition and be compassionate towards her family without supporting their unhealthy behavior. She decided she needed to confront her parents in a loving way. She did not bring up the past or attack her parents. She was not resentful or bitter. She simply pointed out the facts and stated clearly what she felt she could do for the family and what her limits were.

Lena trembled when she talked with her parents, but she knew in her heart that she was doing what was best for everyone.

For the first time in years when Lena finished talking with her parents, she did not feel worthless and resentful. She felt calm, strong and, to her surprise, full of love and compassion for them. She saw that she did not have to abandon herself in order to love her family.

As Lena expected, her parents were angry at her for talking honestly with them. They accused her of not caring for her sister because Lena would not cover Jenny's debts. They resented her "high-handedness" in suggesting they seek help for their drug use. They were clearly shaken by her calm confident manner and her refusal to respond as she had in the past.

When Lena did not back down from her position, her parents saw that her suggestions were practical and necessary. Without a loan from Lena, Jenny and her husband found a financial consultant who helped them manage their debt. They were fortunate to find a progressive and knowledgeable consultant who suggested they go to Debtors Anonymous to treat their compulsive spending.

Lena decided to go to her mother's physician and talk with him about the side effects of her mother's medication. Lena was clear with herself that she would confront the physician and if the medical establishment resisted her, she would let go of the situation.

The physician was willing to support Lena's mother in trying other approaches to her problem. Lena's mother saw a number of specialists and eventually found a way to manage her back pain with diet and exercise and less medication. Once she felt better, Lena's mother insisted that her husband withdraw from Valium and pain medication with the supervision of a physician. His physician was somewhat knowledgeable about addictions. Lena talked with him about her experience with addictions. He was receptive to hearing her and working with Lena to help her father.

Lena faced a final challenge a few days before she left. Her father, who had never thanked her for her help, approached her and said, "Your sister is coming here tomorrow. She's very upset at what's happened. I want you to be nice to her. You've got to learn to be more loving."

Lena had heard this message her entire life and had accepted it as true. This time Lena simply replied, "No, Dad. I don't need to learn to be more loving. I *am* loving. There's nothing I need to do to be 'okay.' Everything I've done on this visit has been loving."

Lena's Christmas visit to her parents was a milestone in her life. She stood up for herself gently but firmly and expressed her love for her family in healthy ways. As she prepared to leave her parents' home she repeated a prayer of gratitude to herself, "Thank you, God, for helping me to heal from my co-dependency. I hate to think what would have happened if I hadn't made the progress I have."

Lena freed herself from the resentment and anger she would have felt if she had gone along with her family's expectations. Instead of reacting as a victim to her family, she grieved that they were unable to accept her and love her in the ways she needed. She accepted that her parents and her sister still suffered from co-dependency, which distorted their love for her. Along with her pain over the family's sickness, Lena felt a renewed love for herself and her family. Although she chose to limit the number and length of her visits with her parents, she did not need to stay completely away from them to maintain a sense of herself. She could feel her deep love for her family and still live from her true self.

Talking About The Past

One reason Lena's visit was so successful is that she followed her intuition and had faith in herself. She decided what actions were appropriate and was willing to feel the emotions that came with her choices. This approach can help you if you are wondering whether to talk with your parents about the past.

Sooner or later most people in recovery ask, "Do I tell my parents everything I'm finding out about my childhood?"

This is a very personal decision. There is no right answer for everyone. It is up to each individual in recovery to decide how to approach his or her parents. Look at what is best for you at a given time. Trust your intuition, talk about your motives with someone who is safe then follow your gut. Remember, you can choose one avenue now and another later in your recovery.

You may choose to address your issues with your parents in person and tell them how you feel about their past behavior. This can be a rewarding experience, even if what you say is not well received. It can be empowering for you to talk honestly about how you experienced your childhood. When you honor your perceptions of your childhood, you enhance your self-esteem, inner strength and clarity.

I have known occasions when people confronted their parents and were shocked at how willing they were to validate what happened in the past. These experiences can be very healing for everyone involved. By breaking the "don't talk" family rule, you and your parents can take an important step towards stopping the disease from being carried on to future generations.

You might choose to do all of your emotional work in therapy and not share your feelings and insights with your parents. You may find this to be the best way to further your recovery. If you feel safe enough, you could also share with people in your 12-Step support groups. There you can find people who understand the issues you are working through and who can honor the feelings you were not allowed to express as a child. It can be healing for you to go through an anger phase during which you have little contact with your parents. As you work on your childhood issues, you can re-evaluate at different stages of your growth whether or not you want to talk with your parents about the past.

You can also choose to heal the wounds from your past in therapy and focus on changing your behavior towards your parents in the present. Standing up to your parents about present-day concerns can be empowering for you. When your parents do something today that you do not like, tell them how you feel in a clear, direct way. As Lena did, stick to the point and hold your ground. Try not to get sidetracked into unrelated issues. Getting away from the issue at hand can often lead to resentment and further enmeshment.

Standing up to your parents may feel uncomfortable at first. You might feel pangs of guilt and fear when you break the rules of your family system by communicating directly. As you become more confident, you will find it easier to tell your parents the truth about how you feel. Often this can lead to unexpected results — when you maintain a sense of yourself and confront your parents in a respectful way, you begin to "unhook" yourself from their influence. This takes time and a commitment to heal your childhood issues. As you become less enmeshed with your parents, you can gradually begin to love your parents for who they are and let go of needing them to change.

If you want to talk with your parents about the past and they are willing to discuss "what went wrong" in the family, I suggest that you approach tender subjects delicately. I have found that in most cases it is not healing to attack parents. Your purpose is to make yourself stronger, but not at the expense of anyone else. You can recover from your co-dependency without showing your parents your pent-up rage and your long-repressed feelings. Rather than telling your parents how bad they were, you can use the communication model we discussed in the previous chapter. You might say, "When you did (tell them about a specific behavior), I felt (share your feeling)." This lets them know that their behavior affected you and how you felt in response.

When the past comes up in conversation, be alert for ways to share responsibly. Paula had many talks about the past with her mother that were supportive and healing.

They both were in recovery and Paula's mother had made it clear that she was receptive to going over the painful parts of Paula's childhood as long as Paula was not abusive.

If your parents are still actively involved in addictions, you need to decide for yourself if confronting them would be best for you. Again trust your intuition. You probably know better than anyone how your parents will respond and what you need to do for your health.

It is helpful to be aware of your motives if you decide to confront your parents on incidents about the past.

Kevin fell into a trap when he confronted his parents. He went through a stage in his late 20s when he railed at his parents for their defective childrearing until he got them to accept their culpability. Then, to his discomfort, it all came back at him. His parents began to tell him, "We know where we went wrong with you. I guess we did really mess you up. It's our fault that you're so unhappy and can't function."

"Wait a minute," Kevin suddenly said to himself, "I'm not totally messed up! I'm not unhappy! I can function!"

Kevin saw his motives. He realized that he had berated his parents about his unhappy childhood to punish them, instead of trying to do what would best further his recovery.

Remember, there is no right and wrong to these issues. I encourage you to go at your own pace. If you talk with trustworthy people and let your inner spirit guide you, you can do what is most healing for you and your family.

Family Visits

Co-dependents usually have a broad range of feelings when they think of visiting their families. As you progress in your recovery and continue to differentiate from your parents, you can turn family visits into times of growth and empowerment rather than regressions to familiar co-dependent ways of behaving. As with most changes in recovery, this is an ongoing process. You will probably grow more confident visiting your family the longer you are in recovery. If you visit your family in the early stages of your recovery, you may struggle to maintain a sense of yourself.

Margaret was in Alcoholics Anonymous for several years before she attended Adult Children of Alcoholics meetings to heal from her dysfunctional childhood. During her years in Alcoholics Anonymous she handled herself more confidently with her family than she had when she was drinking. Even so, after a day or two of being with her family, she would begin to feel anxious and depressed.

These feelings surfaced when she disagreed with someone in her family but did not tell the person how she felt. Her parents had never allowed their children to disagree with them. They would become angry at the slightest difference of opinion from Margaret and her siblings. Margaret was still afraid of their reactions if she shared her opinions honestly. Her fear increased because as she let out her true self, she found that her ideas differed from her family's views more than she had realized.

Margaret's fear of her family's disapproval affected her relationships outside the family. She developed several co-dependent characteristics. She would agree with someone, or give the appearance of agreeing, because she did not want to get into an argument. She was deeply afraid of being verbally attacked. Because she had been intellectually abused by her parents, Margaret felt that most people were smarter than she. This further discouraged her from stating her opinions. She assumed that she would lose any argument she had with another person. If she managed to say something assertive, she couched it in delicate language so that she would not offend anyone.

When Margaret began to attend Adult Children of Alcoholics meetings, she broke the rule of silence in her family. She did not act abusively towards her family or preach about recovery. She simply refused to deny her reality. She learned to disagree with her family and state her opinions clearly. As she honored herself in this way Margaret felt more comfortable visiting her parents, no longer becoming depressed and confused when she visited them. In time Margaret's parents came to respect her for her individuality and were able to have a supportive relationship Margaret had never dreamed was possible.

The Third Generation

When adults play the role of caretaker with their aging parents, they hurt more than themselves and their parents. They model harmful behavior for the next generation — the grandchildren.

The relationship between grandparents and grandchildren can be very special. Because grandparents do not have to discipline the grandchildren on a regular basis, the grandchildren have little to rebel against. Grandparents can be the ones who understand and know the secret desires of your heart. This connection can be a wonderful experience for both young and old.

I have fond memories of my grandparents. These beautiful people were a source of strength and inspiration to me throughout my childhood and all through my life, even after they passed away.

Co-dependency can damage the unique relationship between grandparents and grandchildren. In unhealthy family systems children watch their parents and grandparents misunderstand, resent and abuse one another. Children can be angry at their grandparents for being tyrants, angry at their parents for taking abuse and angry at themselves for going along with the family's behavior.

Anne discovered, to her dismay, how children are affected by the relationship between their parents and grandparents. In Anne's family, as in many co-dependent families, love was defined as helping someone physically without consideration for the person's emotional needs. As long as family members were there for each other physically, it was acceptable to abuse each other emotionally.

Anne's mother had always criticized her, telling her that she could do nothing right. When Anne was physically sick, however, she could count on her mother to be by her side. Anne felt guilty when she thought of confronting her mother about her abuse. She considered herself ungrateful for all that her mother did for her. Anne's fear of standing up to her mother came back to haunt her. When her mother grew older and became sick, Anne took care of her physically, but continued to accept emotional abuse from her mother. Anne believed she was doing what a responsible daughter should do.

Anne's teenage daughter, Lilly, resented the way in which her mother was abused. She saw clearly that her grandmother's behavior was unacceptable. Lilly refused to visit her grandmother. She told her mother, "I wish Grandma would get off your case and just leave us alone. If you're like that when you're older, I'll keep my kids as far away as possible and I sure won't be around to take care of you."

It is possible to heal the distortions of love between the generations. It requires honest communication, clear personal boundaries and a commitment to resolve conflicts. If you are the only one in your family who is trying to change, there may be very little you can do to mend the relationship between you and your grandparents or your children and your parents. However, you may find that as you behave differently, other family members will react to you in new ways. When you open up to the love inside of you, there is a greater chance that the precious loving relationship that is possible between grandchildren and grandparents can grow.

It's Never Too Late

Rhonda had healed many of her issues with her mother. She told me, "My mother was mentally ill most of my life. She was abusive and domineering. Yet she did a lot of good things for our family. She was devoted to us. I felt she was never understood or acknowledged for all she had done. At her funeral I felt sad that she had died without being appreciated.

"Years later, I visited my extended family to gather information for a genealogy and to learn more about my family history. I sensed a feeling of appreciation from my relatives for all my mother had done for them and for her parents. This meant a great deal to me and added to the appreciation I had developed inside of myself for her positive qualities. I began to heal the pain I had felt for so long because of my mother's illness and emotional isolation."

As you continue to separate your identity from your family system, you can begin to see beyond the behaviors that stemmed from your parents' co-dependency, addictions or illnesses. You can become more open to seeing the true person beneath your parents' disease. As long as you pursue recovery and personal growth this process unfolds throughout your life.

One step you can take towards healing with your parents is to begin to look at how your parents were influenced by the social customs of their time. Instead of seeing your parents as rigid or narrow-minded, you may be able to understand that they were simply brought up differently than you and behaved accordingly. This does not make abusive behavior acceptable, but it may help you let go of many of the smaller annoyances and differences in outlook you have with your parents.

When you begin to see your parents in a different light, you may get a sense that they are people with many sides to them. One way to do this is to interview them. Assume the role of an impartial reporter and see what you can learn about their lives. It can be liberating for you to hear how they see themselves beyond their roles as parents. Although being a parent is a central part of their lives, much of who they are has little to do with you. Other people have known them in many different capacities. They see your parents in ways that you may not have seen. Your view of them is likely to be colored. You formed impressions of your parents

when you were very young. You related to them in an
enmeshed family system that bound its members to rigid
rules and expectations. Just as there is more to you than the
role you played in your family, there is more to your parents
than you might expect.

Loni told me about a visit with her parents when she
saw them among a circle of their friends whom she had
not known before. When she saw her parents in this
environment, she realized they were delightful warm people with many strengths.

"I saw that they are wonderful people. They just didn't
know how to be very good *parents*. I saw they had many
nurturing qualities. Lots of people came to see them for
advice and support. Their home was open. People of all
ages visited them — young kids showing them a new
kitten, teenagers asking questions about buying cars,
young adults discussing anxieties about career choices and
friends their age talking about health problems and ways
to help the community.

"I felt angry when I first saw this. I didn't understand
how they could be so good to others when they had been
so negligent to me. I figured they were just putting up a
good front, that people couldn't see them for who they
really were."

Loni shared these feelings in group therapy. As she
healed the deep wounds over not getting the affection she
needed from her parents, Loni was able to appreciate
their redeeming qualities and accept that many people
thought highly of them. She did not have to deny her
experience of them as a child or make her feelings towards
her parents wrong. She was able to accept that *both* could
be true: She had not got what she needed *and* her parents
were very nice people.

Through her work in group therapy Loni freed herself
from a self-destructive pattern that stemmed from her
relationship with her parents. She had often been drawn to
men who were charming and friendly on a social level but
who could not give her the intimacy that she needed. When

she began to accept her parents as they were and let go of expecting them to support her true self, she found she was less attracted to men who were similar to her parents.

"At first it felt strange to change how I saw my parents," Loni said. "I was so used to trying to get more out of them. I saw them be so kind to strangers but not to me. I can still feel the pain of their neglect. When I don't get my needs met by people in my life today, it can trigger this old hurt. The pain only lasts a few minutes and I can move on. As long as I take care of myself, mourn when I need to for the childhood I never had and let go of my parents, my life can be very good. When I live this way, I can accept what my parents do give me. They show their concern through gifts, money and advice. I just have to remember not to be a needy child with them and not to ask for more than they can give."

Loni was able to heal her relationship with her parents, even though they did not change. If one or both of your parents are willing to take the risk to share honestly, together, you may be able to mend much of the hurt between you.

After Morgan's alcoholic father had died, his mother talked more freely about the past. She finally told him all of the family secrets — all of the things she felt she had to keep to herself to protect the family. She talked about the alcoholism, abuse and violence in their family. She told him, "I worried about you so much but I didn't know what to do. I thought it was too horrible to tell you at the time. I felt guilty because I could tell you knew I was hiding things from you. I hope you can forgive me for all I did to hurt you."

Sharing with his mother on this deep level had a powerful effect on Morgan. "I cried my heart out," he said. "I felt a cloud lift from my life. We found the closeness we had never had. I really saw how she had struggled. I realized that I probably couldn't have done it any differently if I had been in her shoes.

"It was challenging to begin to forgive my mother and to move on with my life. I had been comfortable holding on to the wounds of my childhood. The darkness I had felt for so long had become a friend to me. I felt naked and lost without it. As I opened up to my mother and grieved for all those traumatic years, I could see more clearly how it was for my whole family. We were all in a system together, trying to survive in the only ways we knew how. I was grateful that my mother and I had been able to talk so openly before she died. I finally felt in my heart that she really loved me. I cried for all our misunderstandings and pain — for both of us."

A Full Family Reconciliation

The kind of healing that took place between Morgan and his mother can also happen within an entire family. This is less common but as long as the family members are alive, there is always a chance for reconciliation.

Art was married to a woman who devoted most of her time to tennis, golf, bridge, charities and a number of social activities. She spent little time with Art and their four children. The marriage had no emotional life and Art was left to take care of the children most of the time. His wife eventually became involved with another man. She divorced Art and married her lover. Two of the children lived with their father and two lived with their mother.

After the divorce, Art began to drink excessively. A few years later he married Vicki, but his drinking continued. He attended Alcoholics Anonymous meetings several times but after a few weeks of abstinence, went back to drinking. Finally Vicki threatened to leave him unless he stopped drinking. Art went to an in-patient treatment center for his alcoholism and made a clear commitment to change. Vicki went to Al-Anon. They also decided to see me for therapy as a couple.

Despite this new start Art's children continued to attack him for his past behavior. Although they had left home and several had married, they blamed him for all of the family tensions and made him the scapegoat for many of the problems they were having with their lives. To address this situation I agreed to a three-hour family session with Art, Vicki and the four children and their spouses. During the session the sons and daughters expressed their hurt feelings and felt that their father heard them. Art made amends to his children for the pain he had caused them when he was drinking. At the end of the session I said to Art's children,

"Okay, your father has made his amends. He is receptive to hearing your feelings as long as you are not abusive. He is doing everything in his power to recover from his alcoholism and co-dependency. He cannot do anything more about his past behavior. It is time for you to move on. I encourage you to focus on yourselves and take responsibility for your own lives. If you choose, you can recover from your co-dependency just as your father is doing. I can recommend excellent treatment centers, therapists and Adult Children of Alcoholics meetings. I see a lot of hope for this family to heal and grow closer. The choice is up to you."

Art's children responded positively and began to get help for their issues. They no longer dwelled on Art's alcoholism, making him the scapegoat. The family grew closer than it had been in years. Art breathed new air. After this family reconciliation he felt freer to be himself with his children. He began to stand up for himself, state his needs and set limits on what he would tolerate.

Several months after our first meeting, we had another family therapy session. I had each member of the family write a letter to one of his or her parents. In the letters they described how they took care of the parent and shared any feelings that came up. Art and Vicki both wrote to their fathers. Tina, the oldest daughter, had been the most hostile to Art. I encouraged her to write to her mother who had recently died.

The family members read their letters aloud, discussed them and worked through the feelings the letters evoked. When Tina heard Art's and Vicki's letters, she began to see how they had been affected by their families and how the alcoholism and co-dependency had been passed down through the generations. Tina's letter to her mother helped Art and Vicki understand her better. The love among the family members deepened after this session. A few weeks after the session, Tina wrote to thank me for helping her family. She ended the letter by saying, "You gave me my family back. I thought the wounds were too deep and that we would hate each other for the rest of our lives. You showed me that it's never too late."

Your Family History

You can further your recovery by researching your family history. This can be healing for you as well as very exciting. If you can explore beyond your nuclear family and the family myths, you can piece together a fascinating story of the life of a family.

Start by making a *genogram*. This is similar to a family tree except that along with the names of your ancestors, you include as many family events as you can find. See what you can learn about great-grandparents, grandparents, aunts and uncles. Be as honest as you can. Look at divorces, excommunications, suicides, drinking and drug problems and all addictions. Find out about illnesses and causes of death. If you record the truth about your relatives, you will be able to see multigenerational family rules and patterns of behavior that still affect you today.

If you are afraid of how your family will react when you begin to gather this information, I encourage you to take the risk to talk with them. You may be surprised at how open your family will be if you are tactful and approach them in an open nonjudgmental way. Even if there are still family matters considered too delicate to discuss, you can start to uncover much about your family that was not passed down to you in your dysfunctional home. One client told me, "I didn't know my Uncle Colin had spent several years in the Middle East. And my grandmother went to college. She was ahead of her time!"

There will certainly be tender areas that your family may not want to discuss. Alcoholism and other addictions are usually covered up or only referred to in amusing family stories. Many families have been through frightening war experiences and have no desire to recall them. Often, people who have fought in wars choose not to open up about their experiences. It is important to honor these boundaries. You may find that by simply knowing that someone fought in a war, you can gain a fuller picture of that person.

As your parents or grandparents grow older, they may be more willing to share with you. I have a friend who mailed a blank notebook with a pretty cover to each of her grandparents. She included a note saying, "There is so much I wish I knew about you. Please write down whatever you would like about your life." She received back biographies, poetry and anecdotes that gave her a better perspective on herself and her family.

I encourage you to try anything that will teach you more about your family. The more you know of their lives, the more you will understand how you became the person you are. You may see your relatives and yourself as unique, fascinating individuals and feel a deeper empathy for all of your family. As you travel on this journey of discovery your heart will expand and your spirit will continue to grow.

Some Things To Do: Making A List

Write a list of the ways in which you are different from one of your parents. Then write a list of ways in which you are similar to this parent.

The list can include everything from how you arrange your closet to broad philosophical questions. Be sure to include characteristics that relate to intimacy, emotions, self-worth, spirituality and personal values. Try to include traits that you see as both positive and negative.

Then make a list in relation to your other parent.

You can use this information as a kind of personal inventory. It can help you see things about yourself that you may have received from your parents that you appreciate. It may help you see ways in which you would like to differentiate from your parents.

Be gentle with yourself through this process. It is intended to help you be the unique person you are, and to remove whatever is standing in the way of that.

Try to be honest with yourself. In my experience I have found that, indeed, *the truth will set you free.*

PART
III

Love And Recovery

6

Love And Recovery

We have looked at the ways in which your natural empathy and love for others becomes distorted when you are raised in a dysfunctional family system. We have examined the destructive patterns of love, loyalty and caretaking that arise at different stages of your life. Now let's look at what you can do to heal from your past, improve your life today and reclaim your lost heart.

I believe recovery is available for most people and it is up to them to find their own path. Being healthy and functional is an individual experience. People need to discover what is right for them and live according to that. There is no "one way" to health.

You can start to open up to your feelings by loving yourself and taking care of your Inner Child. Taking responsibility for that child's needs and actions and letting him or her express feelings are ways to begin to feel the abundance of love in recovery.

Snowflakes

To begin to reclaim your natural ability to love you can learn to have faith and confidence in the value of your own experience. When you do not value yourself, all the talk in the world about faith, confidence, trusting your Inner Child and changing your life can seem just that — all talk.

Something that has helped me move beyond the talk is a realization about the process of change: You can start with just the slightest crack in the wall, the tiniest moment of serenity or peace within yourself, and build upon it until you have grown into quite a different person.

Years ago I thought I would never experience serenity. I thought it was just not in my temperament to feel at peace. Serenity was just a word to me, not something I had experienced. I had accepted this lack of inner calm as my reality.

One winter's day I was walking home and it began to snow. Big snowflakes floated down, landing on the pavement and lawns. I put out my hands towards the sky and watched the snowflakes fall on them.

A feeling of peace came over me. I was surprised because I had never felt this way before. I had never experienced peace without my anxious thoughts intruding immediately. But now I felt a few moments of serenity for the first time in my life. I told myself, "If I can have this once, I can have it again."

This has turned out to be true. Sometimes I doubted it, but over the years my feeling of serenity has grown. Once I had experienced it, I began to have moments of it more frequently and to accept and rejoice in it when it came. Eventually after years of recovery, serenity became part of who I am. Even when I feel stress pulling on me, the feeling of being at peace deep within myself is there most of the time.

At first it may seem impossible to stand up for yourself and feel good about yourself. Then one day you may briefly experience how it feels — a flicker of self-esteem, a few moments when you see through the heavy weight that you may carry. These moments may be as tiny as a snowflake, but once you experience them, you start the process of change.

As you build trust in opening yourself and letting your feelings gradually evolve, you can begin to *live in the flow*. Your life can become a prayer and a meditation, a daily experience of the Eleventh Step of the 12 Steps of Alcoholics Anonymous. ("Sought through prayer and meditation to improve our conscious contact with God *as we understood Him*, praying only for knowledge of His will for us and the power to carry that out.") Each day you can feel connected with a universal energy.

When you live this way, solutions to your problems seem to appear out of nowhere. You can be more in tune with what you need and want in life. You can ask God/ Goddess to guide your thinking. As you open yourself you can ask, "What would be appropriate in this situation? What should come next?" This may sound simple but it is contrary to all that you probably learned as a child. As we have seen, in a dysfunctional home you learn to always be in control, to always know what you are doing and where you are going. This control is known as *insufficient self-sufficiency*, which keeps you cut off from your greatest resource: your spiritual connection with the Universe.

If you open your heart and ask for guidance, you may be surprised at how much inner direction you will find. You can also be more receptive to wisdom from others. When the words of your family, friends or people you meet resonate with your inner spirit, you can learn from them.

As I grew in my recovery I could tell whether or not I was living in the flow. When I was out of step, my emotions seemed to be a jerky train which tossed me about. When I was going with the flow, my feelings and thoughts felt as though they were rolling smoothly down the track.

When I was off track, I learned to recognize where I was being distracted from the light. I would ask for the ability to see my dark sides and the survival patterns from my past that still interfered with my life. Just as my sense of serenity expanded, my awareness of when I was living from my false self also grew.

Honoring your flow of feelings and who you are at any given moment is a beautiful way to live. You can learn to see your life, and all lives, as sacred. It starts with one small glimmer of light that eventually shines throughout your life each day.

Functional Family Rules

To start or continue on your recovery, you can establish guidelines to help yourself. We discussed the ways in which dysfunctional family rules serve to keep you enmeshed with your family and divided from your true self. In recovery you can write your own rules that support you to be fully alive. To begin with, you can reverse the harmful rules we identified earlier:

1. Feel free to trust with the knowledge that you will become more and more discerning about who is trustworthy.
2. Let yourself feel and share your feelings with others of your choice.
3. Feel free to talk — it is okay to talk about problems, money and sex.
4. Breathe — it is okay to exist.
5. Know what you know.
6. It is okay to not always know what you are doing or where you are going (and it is also okay to know!)
7. Let yourself be vulnerable. You are safe with your inner parent taking care of you.
8. Feel free to need help and to ask for it.
9. Play and be childlike.
10. Feel free to question anyone whose actions and words do not match.
11. Do what you need to do, what feels right to you, instead of the "right thing."
12. Be who you are, instead of trying to be another person's definition of good.
13. Feel free to rock the boat when you need to.
14. Communicate directly and clearly (no need for triangles).

Add to this list any life-supporting guidelines you can think of to affirm your recovery. Remember, you are the adult now and you can choose the guidelines by which you live.

Grief And Learning To Love

Many insightful authors have written about the grieving process. Grief work is an essential part of reclaiming your loving spirit. In fact grieving, with its different phases, such as anger, may be the most important part of therapy. I have found that to fully free yourself from the past, it is necessary to re-experience what you did not allow yourself to feel as a child and mourn the love you did not have.

As Middelton-Moz and Dwinell discuss in their book, *After the Tears*, the essential purpose of allowing yourself to grieve is to work through the repressed trauma of past neglect and abuse. Traumatic childhood experiences would not leave scars and lead to co-dependency and addiction if they could be worked through when they first occur. This is possible if you are raised in a supportive atmosphere with love, open communication and respect for your feelings.

In a dysfunctional home in which feelings are denied, you have no way to process traumatic experiences. This can leave you in a state of chronic shock. The essence of grief work is to allow your Inner Child, the part of you that went through the trauma of an unhealthy childhood, to express his or her feelings at last. This frees you to develop love and empathy for that child, instead of guilt and shame.

Whenever you let go of someone or something, you need to go through a grief process. Often you may try to take short-cuts to avoid your feelings. You may say, "It's God's will, so it's best to just accept it and move on." Others may tell you, "Get hold of yourself and be strong. These things happen to everyone."

One of the most damaging ways to avoid the grief process is to blame yourself and believe that you somehow brought the loss upon yourself. It is important to realize that you did not create trauma and loss in your life as a child. Most of what happens around you at any time is beyond your control. This is especially true for you as a child. If you can mourn your past from the point of view of that innocent child, you can reach the deepest levels of healing.

Middelton-Moz and Dwinell list the common reactions to traumatic experiences. They are:

- Loss, real or threatened.
- Shock, numbness and disbelief.
- Denial, refusal to acknowledge the loss.
- Depression, sadness over the loss.
- Guilt at not having prevented the loss.
- Anger at the loss and our helplessness.
- Resolution.

After The Tears

Breaking through the denial about your past (i.e., "It wasn't that bad") is an important step towards recovery and towards honoring your damaged Inner Child, whose feelings were ignored for so long. As you move through your denial, you free yourself to continue in the grief process. As we will see, this process continues at deeper levels throughout your life. As you learn to honor your feelings and trust in the path of recovery, you can make the grieving process part of the flow of your life. To help you do this, we will look more closely at the world of feelings.

Honoring Your Feelings

If you have never been allowed to express your emotions they may be very frightening to you. As you experiment with your feelings and gather information about how emotions work, you can become more comfortable healing the wounds from your past.

In group therapy sessions Bob became very critical of me when I discussed plans to travel. This was an abandonment issue for Bob. He shared this with me. I honored his feelings and encouraged him to look at who had abandoned him when he was a child. If he had chosen to stay angry at me, he could have blocked his feelings towards his unavailable mother, who later in his childhood became an alcoholic.

Bob recognized that he had this pattern in his romantic relationships. As soon as a woman got too close, he was afraid she would leave him. To avoid his feelings he started to find fault with her and push her away. He would give the woman the double-message: "Come here/ go away." This is a common pattern for co-dependents.

In therapy Bob worked on this avoidance pattern. He got in touch with his pain which originated with his mother. He described the pain as a raw sensation in his solar plexus. When Bob got too close to someone in the present, he felt as though the raw wound was being scraped.

I encouraged Bob to honor his pain, feel it and connect it with images of his mother.

"Hold your Inner Child," I told him. "Imagine holding Little Bob and letting him say, 'I want my mommy.' Just hold him and let the waves of fear and sadness wash over you."

Appropriately enough, Bob's image of his mother was usually of the back of her blouse. Bob also remembered how his mother had taken him for a ride on a horse when he was under two years old. Despite his terrified cries, she showed no regard for his feelings and failed to dialogue with him. From his experience Bob learned not to honor his feelings or his needs, and to put his mother's feelings before his own.

Bob learned to honor his feelings by taking responsibility for his defensive behavior. He learned to catch himself when he had the urge to block his feelings and put up defenses. He learned to say to himself, "Stop! Don't indulge in this defense. It's a signal. Go to the wounded place you're avoiding instead of to the defense. Use this experience to recognize this behavior pattern. It helped you survive in childhood but now you no longer need to defend against intimacy."

When you start to let your feelings out, you may be afraid you will completely lose control and never be able to recover. In fact the opposite is true. Emotions work in a paradoxical way. Emotions naturally come and go quickly. It is the mental act of holding on to them and trying to repress them that prolongs states of depression, anxiety and fear. If you let yourself feel your emotions, they can eventually last only a few minutes (20-30 minutes at the most) before they subside. If you do not allow yourself to have your feelings, you can keep yourself from healing and continue to feel a dull mild pain. If you can go into the wound, feel it and honor it, you will heal it a little more each time.

As we have seen, if you are co-dependent, you will probably do whatever you can to avoid your feelings. Along with turning to the substances and activities to repress your feelings, you can find subtler ways to avoid them. For instance, Phil blocked his anger by telling himself, "I'm childish. I'm oversensitive."

Cynthia, on the other hand, was addicted to anger and felt it all of the time, blocking out every other emotion. It was less painful, less threatening, to feel anger instead of fear, hurt, sadness, betrayal or abandonment. If Cynthia heard a startling noise, such as a door slamming or a car backfiring, she was not frightened. She would become angry — mad at the door or the car for interrupting or persecuting her. Other emotions can mask your true feelings as well. Molly usually felt fear instead of the sorrow that was really in her heart.

To honor your feelings it is important to *stay with them* until you receive the message they are giving you.

As a child, Vince did not receive praise for being strong. It was hard for him to give up being weak and feeling self-pity because he had always been rewarded for being fragile. In therapy I asked him to talk about his parents. I encouraged him to stay in his anger instead of giving in to his urge to cry, which he did often. He felt that his body was too small, too weak to experience strong anger. I told him his body was big enough to contain his anger. Vince learned that there were times to release his anger by shouting in therapy, and other times when he would heal the most by feeling it in his body and simply stating that he was angry.

You can learn to stay with a feeling for a whole day. Eventually you will move through your feeling more quickly. In the beginning of your recovery allow yourself whatever time you need to be with a feeling. You may think, "Oh, I've been angry long enough. I'd better stop this and get on with my life." In fact, you can live your life and still feel the feelings. Try not to let your mind repress your emotions. It is healthiest if your mind and feelings can work together. Wait until you get the message your body is sending you. Anger that lasts more than a few minutes is bound to be telling you something from deep within your childhood. On the other hand, if your anger masks other feelings, you will need to get in touch with what lies beneath the anger. You can experiment with this and find the source of your deepest feelings.

When Howard first allowed himself to experience his repressed feelings, he viewed them as an attack or an emotional storm. He felt ashamed of his feelings and tried to bury them within himself. If something triggered his anger or resentment, Howard would panic. He was afraid he would lose control and not be able to maintain his calm facade. In recovery Howard began to see that he could weather these storms. He could function — go to work, buy food, run errands — and still experience his intense emotions. He learned to make his feelings part of his life and to take care of himself as he felt them.

Eventually Howard realized that in their own way his emotional storms were wonderful experiences. They were eruptions of what he saw as his old personality, left over from his enmeshed childhood.

"This is how I used to be all of the time," he told himself. "Now I'm much healthier. I only have an occasional eruption of old feelings."

These experiences now had a message for Howard. They painted a vivid picture of his past when he had tried to take care of his dysfunctional family system. He saw clearly how his anger and resentment at his powerlessness as a child had tied him to the world of his suffering parents. He could look at these ties and free himself from them with love for himself and his family. All of them deserved better than to live in that enmeshed state.

He added, "The length of these attacks diminished as I better understood them and let them pass through me. At first they may have taken several days, carrying me off on a tidal wave. Now it's usually sharper, one or two hours, sometimes only a few brief minutes."

He also said, "In the beginning I was terrified that I wouldn't survive and that my old personality would reclaim me. Now I see I'm strong enough, compassionate enough, to feel my feelings."

When you first begin recovery and your feelings surface, you can feel overwhelmed. You may need to discharge these feelings in a harmless way, such as shouting or pounding pillows. As you grow you will find that simply releasing the emotion will not necessarily bring about deep healing. You may need to acknowledge the feeling and process it. Ask yourself, "Where am I feeling this in my body? What is the message in my feelings? Who is this in reaction to?" If you can be patient, the answer will usually come. You will be able to learn from your body, move to another level of health and take appropriate actions if necessary.

As you understand your feelings better, you can honor them and still be responsible with them. It is common to think that you must express your anger by letting it flow at the people around you: family, spouses, employers. Although you may be aware that your anger is often displaced from the past and therefore very intense, you may feel you have no choice but to express it. If you let your anger out, you may feel regret when it is out of proportion to the incident in the present that triggered your deep feelings.

When you experience this kind of anger, try not to express it immediately. Take some time in private to feel the emotion. Honor it as your genuine feeling, no matter how irrational it may seem. After you have taken this time, you decide whether or not to express your anger and, if so, how to share it appropriately. Sometimes it is not appropriate to confront a parent, child, lover or friend directly. In such cases you can process your feelings with a support group or therapist.

When you feel strong anger, there is usually a kernel of present-day anger at something a person has done to you, and the rest is the residue of untreated resentment and rage from your past. Most of the time the people with whom you are angry in the present are not doing anything to persecute you, they are simply tending to themselves. They have their own lives that do not center around you.

You can learn to approach other feelings such as emptiness, yearning, restlessness, apathy and despair in this same way. These feelings may seem out of context in the present and bring with them the weight of the past. Instead of expressing your feelings in inappropriate situations, it is more beneficial for you to acknowledge them to yourself and process them in individual or group therapy.

Remember, as you treat your co-dependency, expressing your emotions will become easier and more spontaneous. Suppressing or denying your feelings, especially anger, only prolongs them and stockpiles them. If you let yourself have your feelings, you can heal. Once you do this, you will be surprised at how quickly emotions pass. You will find that your feelings will flow through you in quick waves. Continuing smouldering anger need not be a permanent feature in your emotional landscape.

Give yourself permission to process your emotions at any time. You do not have to express what you feel at the moment, although resolving an issue quickly can be satisfying. However long it takes you to get in touch with a feeling is okay. When you are ready, you can talk with the person with whom you have issues and you can process your feelings in therapy if you need to.

When you begin to express your feelings, you may fear that people will abandon you. You can feel as fearful as when you were a child dependent on your parents for survival. Try to keep in mind that today the threat is different. You might risk losing a friendship, a marriage or the approval of your parents or children. As painful and frightening as this may be, now that you are grown up it is no longer a survival issue. The feelings may be the same but you can ask for support and process them in a safe environment.

You may also find it frightening to live with ambiguity. In a dysfunctional home you grow up believing that there is something wrong with you if you do not understand everything about yourself and your life. You may also fear that something terrible will happen to you if you cannot explain, categorize or rationalize your feelings. But it is a human experience to have different feelings come up at the same time that may not make sense.

A client of mine, Stephanie, learned to accept the ambiguity of her feelings in therapy. Her family often behaved in confusing ways and then got angry with her if she could not immediately tell them what she thought or felt. It helped Stephanie to give herself permission to live for a few hours, a few days, or longer without knowing why she was feeling knotted up inside. She learned to talk with someone, explore her emotions and open herself to all possibilities before deciding what to do.

Remember, being healthy does not mean living free of so-called negative feelings. There are no negative feelings, only interpretations make them so. You can use all feelings to learn about yourself and to further your growth.

Forgiveness

As you honor your feelings and connect them to their source in your childhood, you can begin to truly let go of your parents. You can start on the journey towards forgiveness. Many philosophies and religions encourage you to jump into forgiveness. This can be used as a way to avoid feeling the emotional pain of your past and to make forgiveness strictly a mental exercise. This is not true forgiveness from the heart. Forgiveness is an ongoing process. As you work through your layers of anger and sadness, you can reach deeper levels of forgiveness. This healing process can continue, in some form, throughout your life.

Forgiveness does not imply letting people continue to abuse you. If your parents or other people in your life are abusive, you may choose to relate to them on a limited basis or not at all. But you will be free of your self-destructive resentment. The purpose of forgiveness is to free *you*.

As Earnie Larsen and Carol Larsen Hegarty say,

> "Forgiveness is an act, not a feeling. Though it may generate feelings, forgiveness is an exercise of the will. *When we forgive, we refuse to be further damaged by the wrongdoing of others."*
>
> Days of Healing, Days of Joy

It is important to remember that you can forgive someone and still choose not to relate to them on a personal level. To forgive is to let go of resentment and of the other person. When you let go, you gain another piece of yourself.

Forgiveness is not the same as white-washing someone's behavior. If your parents continue to act abusively, you can refuse to be a target of their disease. As you heal you can feel unconditional love for your parents and others without unconditionally accepting behavior that is not acceptable.

I was taught at an early age to be understanding. I was often told to be understanding of the most bizarre, incomprehensible and intolerable situations. The healthy part of me, the innocent child within me, was angry, sad, lonely, hurt and afraid. She did not understand at all. After years of this indoctrination, however, that child was suppressed in favor of being a "good, understanding" girl. I had learned how to cut myself off from my feelings and live from my head alone.

To recover from this I needed to honor my Inner Child and all she had experienced that was not acceptable. To do this I needed to *not* jump into forgiveness. It was tempting to say, "Well, the past is the past, it's time to forgive and forget." To forgive your parents before you have done deep emotional healing can keep you in co-dependency and further bury your loving spirit. It is safe to say that as long as you do not heal the issues from your family of origin, you will remain untreated.

Recovery is not easy and it is not fast. To fully recover from co-dependency and addictions requires patience and persistence. It is crucial to *blame* until you move through the anger stage of your grief. It is very hard for most co-dependents to get in touch with their anger over the way their parents treated them. And it is even more challenging for them to stay with their anger. As you work through your feelings, you will come naturally to deeper levels of forgiveness. This will be a deep secure feeling, not something you need to convince yourself of.

Awakening Your Body

In many ways co-dependency is a spiritual disease. One way to connect with the spirit, however, is to open yourself on the level of the mind, emotions and body. In fact some form of bodywork with a person who is knowledgeable about co-dependency can be one way to experience a Higher Power in your life. I will not take the time to discuss all of the kinds of bodywork I have found to be healing. I encourage you to look into acupuncture, *Trager* and *Mentastics*, the *Radiance Technique*, Rolfing, shiatsu and Swedish massage.

Trager

Trager work, developed by Milton Trager, can reawaken your body. Trager focuses on maintaining a state of "hook-up." This means being in contact with your Higher Power. When you are in hook-up, you have a sense of universal energy flowing freely through your body, clearing your mind, relaxing and awakening your feelings. A Trager session with a knowledgeable sensitive practitioner who is doing his or her own recovery can be an opportunity for you to practice living fully in the moment and in contact with your Inner Child. Through hook-up you can receive guidance from your Higher Power for self-parenting. Trager work can also provide you with a model for self-validation and emotional health. Working with a practitioner, one on one, gives you a chance to express your needs and to recover from the effects of rules such as "never need help."

My first Trager training was blissful because I was encouraged to make sounds and to move as much as I wanted to. In my family a central rule was: Be quiet and sit still. By receiving permission to make sounds and to move, my Inner Child had a chance to be re-parented in a healthy way. Even receiving a simple compliment such as, "I like your hand," helped to model new affirming behaviors for me. My practitioner was very good at giving me the extra consideration and verbal communication essential to creating a safe environment with full respect for the individual. She encouraged me to give her continuous feedback. She repeatedly reminded me that it was all right to say "no" or "don't do that." I had come from a background in which I was afraid that saying "no" would immediately cause a harmful conflict. Therefore it was a great lesson for me to learn that I could say "no" to any invasiveness and that my fears and boundaries would be respected.

Many co-dependents only experience with touch has been abuse or deprivation. Even a gentle nonintrusive touch may be frightening to you. Trager practitioners can be aware of this and negotiate with you, respectfully dialoguing and letting you slowly open to the experience. When I work with a client using the Trager approach, I sometimes give explicit verbal reassurance, for example, "Sexual feelings may come up and this is normal. You're safe here with me. I'm clear about boundaries." In time you can learn to openly receive touch in a nurturing nonsexual way.

A Trager session may bring up repressed emotions or memories of invasive or abusive physical contact. As you learned to do as a child, you may go numb or "leave your body" so that you don't have to feel buried emotions. A Trager practitioner who is aware of co-dependency issues can see when you begin to go numb and what areas of your body are shut down. I have discovered that the more I understand and heal from the effects of growing up in a dysfunctional family, the more I can intuitively sense the issues that arise for my clients during a Trager session. As I become more aware, I can better help them heal themselves.

I worked on the shoulder of a client, Dale, while he lay on his stomach. As I moved towards his lower back with a steady speed and rhythm he became frightened. I shifted to a careful, delicate touch and one of the dysfunctional family rules occurred to me: Don't rock the boat. I mentioned this to Dale and it triggered memories of walking on eggshells around his alcoholic mother, trying to be quiet and still. Some of the stress from these experiences had been repressed and held in his lower back.

Herb, a Vietnam veteran as well as an adult child of an alcoholic, would become very angry during work on the back of his legs when I moved his left ankle. I discovered the same response when touching his left shoulder. We discovered that his leg had absorbed anger at his mother for hitting him as a child and his shoulder carried the shock of explosions in the war.

Trager and other forms of bodywork are one way to integrate all of the facets of your recovery: opening to your emotions; experiencing healthy, respectful touch and physical intimacy; gently awakening your body from the legacy of abuse and chronic shock; releasing blocked energy and celebrating the joy and passion that can give you a deep healing sense of life, love and spirituality.

Connecting With Your Higher Power

We have looked at the ways in which you may pursue addictions in your search for the fantasy bond with your parents. Beneath your addictions you long for the deep spiritual connection you did not have as a child. Addiction is a pseudo-connection that tries to fill the emptiness inside, that void in you that feels as though the wind can blow right through it. As John Bradshaw says, "Co-de-pendency is the loss of one's inner reality and *an addiction to outer reality.*" (*Bradshaw On: The Family*)

Through your spiritual awareness of a Higher Power, you can begin to reclaim your inner reality and fill your world with meaning and love. I believe your longing for connection is a quest for life. To be fully alive you seek intimacy and connectedness with others, with a special partner, with God/Goddess and with your own heart. In recovery these levels of connectedness can replace the loneliness of addiction.

Finding your spiritual connection in the world is a very personal, subjective experience. The beauty of spirituality is that there is no "right" path for everyone. You can describe the experience of opening to your Higher Power in any way that feels true to you. According to Virginia Satir,

"Spiritual power can be seen in a person's reverence for life — hers and all others, including animals and nature, with a recognition of a universal life force referred to by many as God."

Quoted in **Each Day A New Beginning**

I believe that you can only truly know your relationship with a Higher Power through yourself — through your feelings, sensations and awareness. This is reflected in the 12-Steps of Alcoholics Anonymous that refer to "God *as we understood Him.*" Institutions and other people cannot give you this knowingness, you need to experience it for yourself. It is this personal experience that heals.

For me, a Higher Power is something greater than us that connects with our spirit — with the sacred, pure, innocent part of our souls. This part of us is unharmed and untainted by the disease of co-dependency. I have learned to open up and let that greater power come in and touch the deepest part of me. For me, it is this connection that is healing and that renews my sense of love in life.

The relationship between you and a spiritual force is reciprocal. As you get to know yourself better, you will develop a deeper sense of your Higher Power; as your spirituality grows, so will your self-knowledge.

As you grow and open to your true self, you are more open to *feeling* the love and connection with the Spirit of the Universe. In time your spirituality can become an actual physical sensation. This is not an abstract left-brain experience. It is also not an addictive feeling. Spiritual awareness is feeling free and fully present with the universe and other people. It is a peaceful, yet exciting, sensation of energy. It is an aliveness in your body that brings you a sense of meaning and purpose in life and opens you to live free of addiction — in your relationships and in all areas of your life.

The maturity of your relationship with God/Goddess is akin to the maturity and commitment of love. There will be times when your *feeling awareness* of your Higher Power fades or only passes through you fleetingly. This is when you need to trust and turn to the strength of your commitment to spirituality, just as you commit yourself in an intimate relationship. This is a sign of spiritual maturity.

Although your spiritual quest can lead you to abundance, it may start with a feeling of emptiness. Your spirituality can grow on acceptance of the inner mystery you encounter when you let go of your familiar dysfunctional behavior and the unhealthy drama that has filled your life. This can be a difficult step to take. If you are co-dependent, you may have said to yourself, "I am the person who coped with the drama, who has survived the abuse. That is my identity. When the people who abused me are gone, when the crisis and the drama are over, what's left of me?"

You may feel that the answer is, "Not very much." As we have seen, you may avoid this frightening feeling by recreating the same crisis, drama and abuse of your childhood in your adult relationships. In recovery you reach a point at which you need to begin building a new healthy identity. You can summon the courage to walk through the emptiness, the loneliness, the times you feel you do not have an identity. Connection with a Higher Power can help you to find out who you really are, little by little.

Arnold found that when he first let go of his compulsive urge to avoid conflict, he was not sure of how he felt about anything. He went through a frightening period when he was ashamed of not knowing what he liked, even in the most trivial things. He could not even answer a question such as, "What's your favorite flavor of ice cream?" He had always told people, "I like everything," out of fear of offending someone. Now his true feelings were a mystery to him. When he accepted this, he felt free to begin to experience and delight in self-discovery.

Stan also faced a terrifying emptiness. He realized that without the compulsive need to perform, to show off and win approval, he felt unmotivated to do anything. He had always been a keen competitor in business and a sharp dresser, trying to win women's approval. In his recovery Stan did not feel a desperation to succeed in business or to dress up. There was no longer a constant inner pressure telling him how to behave. Without this compulsion to guide him Stan felt paralyzed. He was unable to continue with those parts of his life that he had compulsively built up. Stan found the courage to let himself live in this emptiness. Eventually he learned to listen to his inner voice and to be spiritually guided. He was then able to understand the mystery of pursuing interests out of enjoyment, happiness and love.

As you open yourself to your connection with a spiritual force in the universe, you will give your true self the support to come out of hiding. You can mature spiritually and emotionally, as your self-knowledge and awareness of your Higher Power grow together.

The Lifelong Commitment

"And the issue can't be whether or not it will hurt; it will. The issue is — which path will take us where we want to go, one step at a time? . . . Today, I pray for the courage to live

with inner conflict. I will not frustrate myself by expecting
recovery to be easy."

Earnie Larsen and Carol Larsen Hegarty
Days of Healing, Days of Joy

At times the journey in recovery can be so painful, the
darkness so deep, that you may feel it is too much to go
through. During the darker moments you may feel tempted to return to your addictions and self-destructive behaviors and to avoid taking responsibility for your life.
When you grieve deeply for your past, the pain can be
gut-wrenching. It takes tremendous courage to look at
your past, to feel your feelings, to take risks and to share
your feelings with others.

It is my experience that the only way out is in. To truly
heal from your past you need to journey back and experience the feelings that have been buried for so many
years. As Marcel Proust wrote, *"We are healed of a suffering
only by experiencing it to the full."* It is only by finally honoring
and processing your feelings that you will be able to free
your true self. On this inner journey I have found layers
of darkness that I have needed to experience and to get to
know if I wanted true light and clarity. This process has
unfolded in waves over time and has had a life of its own.

Through this healing process love sustains — self-love
and love for all creatures. Love cures. It supports you
while you are in conflict. When you stay with love a
deeper space opens inside of you to heal, to be in a greater
peace beyond the pain.

I do not believe that it is healing to force this process.
Instead you can pursue recovery and trust that your
Higher Power is guiding your path. You can try to live as
best you can, allowing for mistakes, regressions and confusion. You can make your life a healing journey by taking
each day as an opportunity and a challenge to learn about
yourself and others.

An important step you can take for your recovery is to
have the *intention* of a lifelong commitment to be lived one
day at a time: an intention to be healthy, to grow and to

care for yourself. *Recovery is self-care and self-responsibility.* It is growing up! It is now up to you to parent yourself, make the choices that are best for you.

In your recovery you need to be willing to support yourself, no matter who you are involved with or you will go under. Watch how you may abuse yourself subtly by not taking care of yourself. If you can stay focused on self-nurturing and self-responsibility, you may find it helpful to your growth.

As you learn to care for yourself it is helpful to understand what is meant by practicing *tough love* on others and on yourself. The people you love and wish to care for may need to suffer as part of their emotional growth. If they are co-dependent and addicted, they will usually need treatment. They must find their Inner Child and mourn their past in order to grow. You cannot do it for them. When you do for them what they need to do for themselves, you enable them to stay sick. You allow them to avoid the pain that can help them to seek recovery. You can show true love for the people in your life by supporting them to find recovery and by not buying into their misery, denial and "poor me" stories. For a time you may need to be tough on yourself too by not buying into your own self-pity.

After reading this book, you may have a better understanding of the co-dependent's *dilemma of love.* I hope that I have helped you sort through some of your confusing feelings of guilt, loyalty and compassion. We have seen that taking care of other people's needs at your expense is usually not a true healthy expression of love and empathy. And taking care of a family system that lives by a set of dysfunctional rules, trapping its members in enmeshment and rigid behaviors, will keep you in the disease of co-dependency.

It takes time to learn to trust yourself and to learn to love in healthy ways. As you free yourself from addictions and heal your underlying co-dependency, you will find that healthy love will come more naturally from within. In recovery you can begin to trust yourself and others. Little by little you will be able to judge for yourself when and where it is safe to open up and notice if indeed it has been safe before you share more of yourself. You do not need to abandon yourself any more.

Once you open up your heart you will begin to reclaim your true self: the loving person you have always been but who needed to hide from the world in order to survive. You no longer need to hide. You are safe today. You can now be your own nurturing parent. Your Inner Child is finally free to be fully alive and fully loving.

Some Things To Do:
"Letters . . . " And Affirmations

Unprocessed and unfinished grief can be a block to being fully alive and to being fully present with yourself and others. To help you in the grief process and to validate what happened to you as a child, try writing a letter to your Inner Child.

You can start the letter with: "Dear _____" and fill in your name. If there is a special name by which your Inner Child would like to be called, see how it feels to use that name.

Tell your Inner Child about the people and events from your past that you still need to grieve. Tell him or her the truth about what happened in your dysfunctional family.

Ask your Inner Child to write to you and tell you what he or she experienced and share any feelings with you. You can reassure your Inner Child that it is safe to tell you all about it today.

If you want, you could make the letter as simple as:

Dear Little Susan,

I feel I have a lot of grieving to do about what happened to us in the past. It is now safe for you to tell me everything you experienced and how you feel about it. Could you do that for me?

Love,
Susan

When your Inner Child is ready to write to you use the hand you usually do not write with.

You can address this letter to your adult: "Dear _____ _____ " and fill in your name.

Let your Inner Child tell you about anything that happened to him or her and about unresolved issues with people from the past. If you can, allow your Inner Child to have any feelings that come up and nurture him or her. You can continue to reassure your Inner Child that it is safe to share and feel today. He or she is finally safe and on the path to openness, love and health.

Affirmations

Try saying these affirmations to yourself in the morning and at night. If you can, look at yourself in the mirror when you say them and see if you can truly honor the person you see. Try to allow yourself to take in the affirmations.

1. *I am a precious human being who cannot be replaced on this planet.*

2. *There is only one me and I am responsible to nurture my gifts and to let my light shine.*

3. *I am in charge of my life and the path I choose.*

4. *My first priority is my own well-being and the journey of my soul.*

5. *I am responsible for my attitudes, feelings and behavior. I do not assume responsibility for those of others.*

6. *As my behavior becomes more appropriate, my success grows.*

7. *I am a fallible human being who makes mistakes. I learn from my mistakes and am accountable for them.*

8. *I am not inferior or superior to anyone else.*

9. *I deserve to be treated with dignity.*

10. *I am gentle and loving to myself.*

11. *I am patient with myself.*

12. *There is plenty of time. I have the rest of my life to continue to grow.*

Final Thoughts:
Notes On Therapy

A book is, of course, no substitute for deep work with a knowledgeable therapist. All that we have discussed in this book, however, can help you to find a therapist who will best benefit your recovery.

When you meet a potential therapist, try to get a sense of whether you and the therapist are compatible. If you are not compatible, I suggest you find another one.

I also encourage you to ask the therapist if he or she is co-dependent and is knowledgeable in treatment of the disease. You would want to know what sort of recovery the therapist has undertaken. It would not benefit you to work with an untreated therapist. As we discussed earlier, co-dependents are often drawn to caretaking roles and to adopt the image of a caretaker. It has been estimated that a large percentage of people in the helping professions come from co-dependent backgrounds.

For your greatest healing you will also want to know if the therapist understands the importance of freeing yourself from addictions, in addition to healing from your underlying disease of co-dependency. If you continue to act on your addictions, you will not be able to reach the deepest levels of grief and release of shame that are necessary for your full recovery.

It is a good idea to interview several therapists, unless you have an excellent recommendation. It is helpful to remind yourself that a therapist will learn about the deepest and most vulnerable parts of who you are. This is why you need a person who takes his or her own recovery seriously.

Because co-dependency results from unhealthy relationships, the way you and your therapist relate is central to your recovery. When you recover in relation to someone who is healthy, you can learn to interact in life-affirming ways. Your therapist can model healthy interpersonal behavior for you. To be able to do this with you, a therapist must have done intense family of origin work.

One of the most effective ways I have found to heal from severe co-dependent shame is through group work. If you can talk about your experiences, particularly sexual exploitation and abuse, and see that the group members do not react to you negatively, you can slowly get over your shame. It is very healing to reveal shameful secrets and see that the people in your group still care about you, respect and honor you. This can be more healing than individual therapy. For this reason, if you must choose between individual and group therapy, I recommend the group experience, although I believe both are important.

It is also important to avoid turning therapy into a new addictive process. If you are just starting to attend a support group, such as Alcoholics Anonymous, you will probably need to attend meetings quite a lot. It is recommended that people attend every day for the first 90 days of their recovery. As you grow in recovery and work in individual and group therapy, you can attend fewer 12-

Step meetings. You must find your own balance between meetings and living life.

It is very important for you to always remember that, as much as a therapist needs to stress your accountability as an adult, under no circumstances would you want to work with someone who holds you in any way responsible for the events of your childhood.

For instance, if a therapist asks you to look at your part in the incest of your childhood, leave the office as fast as you can! That therapist clearly does not understand the nature of this abuse. Any therapist who thinks this way has most likely not healed his or her family of origin issues. It needs to be a given in your therapy that you were helpless as a child. You were at the mercy of adults. You were never the cause of abuse and you never deserved to be abused, regardless of your actions, thoughts or feelings. The minute you start to blame yourself for your parents' abuse towards you, you are out of the recovery process and into the disease of co-dependency. You are grasping at the illusion of control that keeps you from experiencing the pain and terror of your helplessness as a child.

Be sure to look into a 12-Step program. These programs help you heal the addictions that spring from the underlying disease of co-dependency. As we have seen, freeing yourself from addiction is central to full recovery from co-dependency.

The 12-Step programs can help you stay connected with the spiritual force in the world. They can also help you to accept yourself and your fallibility, as well as to accept other people. Through the 12-Steps you can free yourself from perfectionism and gain greater flexibility in your life. You can learn to be kind and gentle with yourself, to interact with others with respect and dignity.

I encourage you to do whatever you can to help yourself in your recovery. Try not to despair. You can find help, growth and love. Take the risk!

If you commit yourself to recovery I think you will find the words of Thoreau to be true:

"I learned this, at least, by my experiment; that if one advances confidently in the direction of his dreams, and endeavors to live the life which he has imagined, he will meet with a success unexpected in common hour."

Walden

APPENDIX I

The Twelve Steps
Of Alcoholics Anonymous

1. We admitted we were powerless over alcohol — that our lives had become unmanageable.
2. Came to believe that a Power greater than ourselves could restore us to sanity.
3. Made a decision to turn our will and our lives over to the care of God *as we understood Him.*
4. Made a searching and fearless moral inventory of ourselves.
5. Admitted to God, to ourselves, and to another human being the exact nature of our wrongs.
6. Were entirely ready to have Him remove all these defects of character.
7. Humbly asked Him to remove our shortcomings.
8. Made a list of all persons we had harmed, and became willing to make amends to them all.
9. Made direct amends to such people wherever possible, except when to do so would injure them or others.
10. Continued to take personal inventory and when we were wrong promptly admitted it.

11. Sought through prayer and meditation to improve our conscious contact with God *as we understood Him*, praying only for knowledge of His will for us and the power to carry that out.

12. Having had a spiritual awakening as a result of these steps, we tried to carry this message to alcoholics, and to practice these principles in all our affairs.

The 12 Steps are reprinted with the permission of Alcoholics Anonymous World Services, Inc.

APPENDIX II

Co-dependency And ACoA Treatment Centers*

Caron Foundation Family Services
P.O. Box A Galen Hill Road
Wernersville, PA 19565
tel. (215) 678-5267

5-day in-patient

Center for Problem Resolution
Suncoast Hospital
1793 Penelope Lane
Largo, FL 34644
tel. (813) 586-7118
    (813) 585-9986

21-day and 28-day
in-patient

Choices Counseling Center
P.O. Box 144
Winter Park, FL 32790
tel. (305) 628-3443

5-day in-patient

Halterman Center
Madison County Hospital
210 North Main St.
London, OH 43140
tel. (614) 852-1372 x500

28-day in-patient

The Meadows   4-6 week in-patient, and
P.O. Box 97   5-day workshops:
Wickenburg, AZ 85358   "Survivors I" and
tel. (602) 684-2815   "Survivors II"
    1-800-621-4062

Onsite Training and Consulting, Inc.   8-day in-patient and
2820 West Main St.   6-day reconstruction
Rapid City, SD 57702
tel. (605) 341-7432
Sharon Wegscheider-Cruse

Self-Discovery
Randolph County Hospital
1000 Wadley Highway 22
Roanoke, AL 36274
tel. (205) 863-4111

Sierra Tucson   30-day in-patient,
33 W. Ft. Lowell, Suite 123   and 5-day out-patient
Tucson, AZ 85705   as a Family Workshop
tel. (602) 792-4792   participant
    1-800-624-9001 x2055 (o/s AZ)
    1-800-624-4624 (in AZ)

Triad Recovery Center   5-day in-patient, and
P.O. Box 2081   ongoing out-patient
Middletown, CT 06457
tel. (203) 346-6787

---

* Several of these also address chemical dependency, eating disorders, sexual issues and other addictions. Please contact them directly. They will be glad to send you information.

SELECTED READING

Black, Claudia. **It Will Never Happen to Me.** Denver, CO: M.A.C., Printing and Publications Div., 1982.

Boszormenyi-Nagy, Ivan and Spark, Geraldine M. **Invisible Loyalties.** Hagerstown, MD: Harper & Row, 1973.

Bradshaw, John. **Bradshaw On: The Family.** Pompano Beach, FL: Health Communications, 1988.

_____. **Healing The Shame That Binds You.** Deerfield Beach, FL: Health Communications, 1988.

Bowen, Murray. **Family Therapy in Clinical Practice.** New York: Jason Aronson, 1978.

_____. "Theory in the Practice of Psychotherapy." In **Family Therapy,** edited by Phillip J. Guerin. New York: Gardner Press, 1976.

Carnes, Patrick. **Out of the Shadows: Understanding Sexual Addiction.** Minneapolis, MN: CompCare Publishers, 1983.

Each Day a New Beginning. New York: Harper/Hazelden, Harper & Row, 1985.

Earll, Bob. **I Got Tired of Pretending.** Tucson, AZ: STEM Publications, 1988.

Firestone, Robert and Catlett, Joyce. **The Fantasy Bond.** New York: Human Sciences, 1987.

Fossum, Merle A. and Mason, Marilyn J. **Facing Shame.** New York: W. W. Norton, 1986.

Gorski, Terence. "Addictive Relationships." Independence, MO: Herald House/Independence Press, audiocassette, 1987.

Kritsberg, Wayne. **Adult Children of Alcoholics Syndrome.** Pompano Beach, FL: Health Communications, 1986.

Larsen, Earnie. **Stage II Recovery: Life Beyond Addiction.** San Francisco, CA: Harper & Row, 1985.

Larsen, Earnie and Hegarty, Carol Larsen. **Days of Healing, Days of Joy.** Center City, MN: Hazelden Foundation, 1987.

Mellody, Pia. **Facing Codependence: What It Is, Where It Comes From, How It Sabotages Our Lives.** San Francisco, CA: Harper & Row, 1989.

Middelton-Moz, Jane and Dwinell, Lorie. **After The Tears.** Pompano Beach, FL: Health Communications, 1986.

Miller, Alice. **The Drama of the Gifted Child.** New York: Basic Books, 1981.

_____. **For Your Own Good.** New York: Farrar, Strauss, Giroux, 1983.

Schaef, Anne Wilson. **When Society Becomes An Addict.** San Francisco, CA: Harper & Row, 1987.

_____. **Escape From Intimacy.** San Francisco, CA: Harper & Row, 1989.

Subby, Robert. **Lost In The Shuffle.** Pompano Beach, FL: Health Communications, 1987.

Wegscheider-Cruse, Sharon. **Choicemaking.** Pompano Beach, FL: Health Communications, 1985.

_____. **Coupleship.** Deerfield Beach, FL: Health Communications, 1988.

_____. "Co-dependency: The Trap and the Triumph." Rapid City, SD: Nurturing Networks, audiocassette, 1986.

_____. **Another Chance.** Palo Alto, CA: Science and Behavior, 1981.

_____. **The Miracle Of Recovery.** Deerfield Beach, FL: Health Communications, 1989.

Other Books By . . .
Health Communications, Inc.

ADULT CHILDREN OF ALCOHOLICS
Janet Woititz
Over a year on *The New York Times* Best-Seller list, this book is the primer on Adult Children of Alcoholics.
ISBN 0-932194-15-X   **$6.95**

STRUGGLE FOR INTIMACY
Janet Woititz
Another best-seller, this book gives insightful advice on learning to love more fully.
ISBN 0-932194-25-7   **$6.95**

DAILY AFFIRMATIONS: For Adult Children of Alcoholics
Rokelle Lerner
These positive affirmations for every day of the year paint a mental picture of your life as you choose it to be.
ISBN 0-932194-27-3   **$6.95**

CHOICEMAKING: For Co-dependents, Adult Children and Spirituality Seekers — Sharon Wegscheider-Cruse
This useful book defines the problems and solves them in a positive way.
ISBN 0-932194-26-5   **$9.95**

LEARNING TO LOVE YOURSELF: Finding Your Self-Worth
Sharon Wegscheider-Cruse
"Self-worth is a choice, not a birthright", says the author as she shows us how we can choose positive self-esteem.
ISBN 0-932194-39-7   **$7.95**

BRADSHAW ON: THE FAMILY: A Revolutionary Way of Self-Discovery
John Bradshaw
The host of the nationally televised series of the same name shows us how families can be healed and individuals can realize full potential.
ISBN 0-932194-54-0   **$9.95**

HEALING THE CHILD WITHIN:
Discovery and Recovery for Adult Children of Dysfunctional Families
Charles Whitfield
Dr. Whitfield defines, describes and discovers how we can reach our Child Within to heal and nurture our woundedness.
ISBN 0-932194-40-0   **$8.95**

Enterprise Center, 3201 S.W. 15th Street,
Deerfield Beach, FL 33442
1-800-851-9100

Health
Communications, Inc.

Books from . . .
Health Communications

AFTER THE TEARS: Reclaiming The Personal Losses of Childhood
Jane Middelton-Moz and Lorie Dwinnel
Your lost childhood must be grieved in order for you to recapture your
self-worth and enjoyment of life. This book will show you how.
ISBN 0-932194-36-2   **$7.95**

HEALING YOUR SEXUAL SELF
Janet Woititz
How can you break through the aftermath of sexual abuse and enter into
healthy relationships? Survivors are shown how to recognize the problem
and deal effectively with it.
ISBN 1-55874-018-X   **$7.95**

RECOVERY FROM RESCUING
Jacqueline Castine
Effective psychological and spiritual principles teach you when to take
charge, when to let go, and how to break the cycle of guilt and fear that
keeps you in the responsibility trap. Mind-altering ideas and exercises will
guide you to a more carefree life.
ISBN 1-55874-016-3   **$7.95**

ADDICTIVE RELATIONSHIPS: Reclaiming Your Boundaries
Joy Miller
We have given ourselves away to spouse, lover, children, friends or
parents. By examining where we are, where we want to go and how to get
there, we can reclaim our personal boundaries and the true love of
ourselves.
ISBN 1-55874-003-1   **$7.95**

RECOVERY FROM CO-DEPENDENCY:
It's Never Too Late To Reclaim Your Childhood
Laurie Weiss, Jonathan B. Weiss
Having been brought up with life-repressing decisions, the adult child
recognizes something isn't working. This book shows how to change
decisions and live differently and fully.
ISBN 0-932194-85-0   **$9.95**

SHIPPING/HANDLING: All orders shipped UPS unless weight exceeds 200 lbs., special routing is requested, or
delivery territory is outside continental U.S. Orders outside United States shipped either Air Parcel Post or Surface
Parcel Post. Shipping and handling charges apply to all orders shipped whether UPS, Book Rate, Library Rate, Air
or Surface Parcel Post or Common Carrier and will be charged as follows. Orders less than $25.00 in value add
$2.00 minimum. Orders from $25.00 to $50.00 in value (after discount) add $2.50 minimum. Orders greater than
$50.00 in value (after discount) add 6% of value. Orders greater than $25.00 outside United States add 15% of
value. We are not responsible for loss or damage unless material is shipped UPS. Allow 3-5 weeks after receipt of
order for delivery. Prices are subject to change without prior notice.

Enterprise Center, 3201 S.W. 15th Street,
Deerfield Beach, FL 33442
1-800-851-9100

**Health
Communications, Inc.**

Daily Affirmation Books from . . .
Health Communications

GENTLE REMINDERS FOR CO-DEPENDENTS: *Daily Affirmations*
Mitzi Chandler
With insight and humor, Mitzi Chandler takes the co-dependent and the adult child through the year. Gentle Reminders is for those in recovery who seek to enjoy the miracle each day brings.
ISBN 1-55874-020-1 $6.95

TIME FOR JOY: *Daily Affirmations*
Ruth Fishel
With quotations, thoughts and healing energizing affirmations these daily messages address the fears and imperfections of being human, guiding us through self-acceptance to a tangible peace and the place within where there is *time for joy.*
ISBN 0-932194-82-6 $6.95

CRY HOPE: *Positive Affirmations For Healthy Living*
Jan Veltman
This book gives positive daily affirmations for seekers and those in recovery. Everyday is a new adventure, and change is a challenge.
ISBN 0-932194-74-5 $6.95

SAY YES TO LIFE: *Daily Affirmations For Recovery*
Father Leo Booth
These meditations take you through the year day by day with Father Leo Booth, looking for answers and sometimes discovering that there are none. Father Leo tells us, "For the recovering compulsive person God is too important to miss — may you find Him now."
IBN 0-932194-46-X $6.95

DAILY AFFIRMATIONS: *For Adult Children of Alcoholics*
Rokelle Lerner
Affirmations are a way to discover personal awareness, growth and spiritual potential, and self-regard. Reading this book gives us an opportunity to nurture ourselves, learn who we are and what we want to become.
ISBN 0-932194-47-3
(Little Red Book) $6.95
(New Cover Edition) $6.95

Enterprise Center, 3201 S.W. 15th Street,
Deerfield Beach, FL 33442
1-800-851-9100

Health Communications, Inc.

THE MAGAZINE FOR AND ABOUT ...

ADULT CHILDREN OF ALCOHOLICS

WE UNDERSTAND. . .

. . . what it means to be the child of an alcoholic. We know the confusion, the intense self-criticism, the bottled-up anger you carry with you. You are not alone.

How do we know? Because we, like you, are part of the 28 million Americans who are children of alcoholics. And we have seen our numbers grow into a social movement focused on the special needs and understanding of people like us.

Changes . . . The Magazine For and About Children of Alcoholics, is part of the new vision of hope for CoAs everywhere. The understanding that comes from caring can lead to healing. But none of us can do it alone. We need each other. The isolation, desolation and despair of the alcoholic family is not all that binds us. It is the hope — and the truth — that things will get better.

We hope you share in the vision by subscribing to *Changes* . . . For and About Children of Alcoholics. It's a change for the better.

☐ **YES** . . . Send my subscription to the following address:
☐ 1 Year (6 Issues) . . . $18.00   ☐ 2 Years (12 Issues) . . . $34.00

Your Name: _____

Address: _____
_____

Payment Form (Check One):
☐ Check or Money Order Enclosed (Payable to The U.S. Journal)
☐ M.C. #: _____ Exp. Date: _____
☐ VISA #: _____ Exp. Date: _____

Agency P.O.'s & Vouchers accepted. Attach documentation for billing purposes.

Cardholder's Signature: _____

The U.S. Journal, Inc., 3201 S.W. 15th Street, Enterprise Center
Deerfield Beach, FL 33442 • 1-800-851-9100